ANDREW SHAW

The New Mom's Guide to New Dads

First edition

Cover art by Fe Amarante
Proofreading by Natalie Silver

This book was professionally typeset on Reedsy.
Find out more at reedsy.com

Contents

Dedication

To my incredible wife, who makes things look easy and has the patience of at least, like, five saints.

To Elliott, Hannah, and Quinn, who say "I love you" when I need to hear it most and who make me laugh all the time.

To my parents, for being excellent role models. Even if I refused to eat vegetables for years.

To my in-laws, for cheering on this book journey every step of the way.

To all of the parents I've met along the way, for offering me advice and guidance, for listening to me and for supporting me as I worked on this book. Thank you so much.

*You know what it's like having five kids? Imagine
you're drowning. And someone hands you a baby.*

— Jim Gaffigan

1

We have no idea how to be a dad.

He's been told his whole life that being a dad is expensive, awkward, gross and overwhelming.

I love *Mr. Holland's Opus.*

I always watch it when it's on TV. The Richard Dreyfuss movie revolves around a beloved music teacher who wanted to be a composer but ended up spending his career at a high school balancing work and his new role as a dad.

I think we can all agree that each of us should try to do so well in our careers that we get a "Mr. Holland Moment" in which people are so moved by what we've done that they orchestrate an elaborate ceremony to celebrate our accomplishments. I can only hope that one day my six-year old-son, Elliott, and my four-year-old twins, Hannah and Quinn, will coordinate an elaborate ceremony in my honor.

As a father, however, is Mr. Holland a worthy role model?

Not even close. Not that the movie makes it seem that way. Like many dads in pop culture, the bar is set very, very low and, whether he realizes it or not, your partner is getting a lot of unintentional direction on what fatherhood is all about from these types of sources.

Here's the takeaway your partner could get from watching *Mr. Holland's Opus*:

- Becoming a dad will destroy your hopes and dreams and force you to take a job you loathe.
- Becoming a dad means a lot of fights with your wife over how you can't pursue your dreams (in his case, writing songs) and be a good dad at the same time.
- Being a dad is expensive (his son is deaf and has to go to an expensive school).
- Fatherhood is about dealing with disappointment, especially related to how your kid negatively affects your life.

These are subtle themes, but they are representative of the overarching theme you'd see in most any movie, television show or song related to being a dad. (In fact, think of how many plots are based on an absent or cruel father. Most Disney movies, in fact.)

That's the thing: While motherhood is often presented as a rewarding, life-improving, loving journey, fatherhood is portrayed as just the opposite, even though it can be incredibly enriching and life-defining in the best possible way.

> *Fatherhood is presented in pop culture as a thing to overcome or accommodate. Motherhood is presented as a state of being to which a woman should aspire.*

You're preparing for motherhood now, either as a mom-to-be

or as a new mom just learning the ropes. Based on how society trains young boys and girls for adulthood, it's likely you are coming into the whole parenting thing with a different set of values and preconceptions about what your new role will be like compared to your partner.

You've been handed dolls since you were a little girl, and it was just assumed you'd be interested in taking care of a fake baby (kind of a big assumption in hindsight, right?!). For a little boy to do likewise, it would be a thing. That's messed up but true. If your son wanted to carry a baby doll, nosy strangers would find it peculiar.

Strangers are the worst, especially when you're a new parent. There are so many unsolicited opinions. I'm sure that if it wasn't for all of our collective fears of the opinions of people we don't even know, we would be much more confident as parents.

My wife and I sometimes throw coats on our kids for the three seconds they're walking from the car to the store in 50-degree weather because (and this has happened!) someone would otherwise give us shit for letting our kids be cold.

I remember when my then-infant son had pooped through his clothes in the grocery store parking lot and I had to change him in the front seat. Some lady on my way into the store made sure to loudly comment, "A little cold out to not be wearing a jacket!"

Gee, thanks. I hadn't thought of that.

It's not a leap to assume she figured a dad alone with a baby wouldn't think to grab a coat.

There are lower expectations for guys.

Just the same, we, in American culture, expect women to be familiar and comfortable with babies, even if you've never held one before. That's undue pressure on you, to say the least. You're just making this stuff up as you go, and even if you babysat as a teenager, have a baby nephew or work with kids for a living, motherhood is a whole new world.

Women I've spoken to have said that they've been talked to for years as though their eventual motherhood is a foregone conclusion. Does that sound familiar? Doubly so if you're young and married. TRIPLE if you're slightly older and married and financially stable.

I have married couple friends who decided kids weren't for them, and they have to constantly explain that no, it's not a medical thing — they just don't want a baby. (Or even if it is a medical thing, it's not your business!) As though they've done something wrong when in fact a child-free life is absolutely right for them.

You know how it goes as you get older:

1. Single: When are you going to find someone?
2. In a relationship: When are you getting married?
3. Married: When are you having a baby?
4. Have a baby: When are you having another baby?
5. Have seven babies: Good God, why so many babies? Ever heard of birth control?

People naturally assume you will keep progressing to the next step in what we as a society have agreed is the "norm," whether that works for you or not.

Emphasis here is on "you will." Once the guy proposes, the onus shifts to the woman to keep that chain of events moving. It may take two to make a baby, but guys are not often asked passive aggressively why they don't have a baby yet. Why not? Shouldn't they have to endure the same expectations?

It goes back to our philosophy of success.

Male success is first viewed within the prism of careers. Female success is first viewed within the prism of raising a family.

Notice I said first. Men and women, of course, can be viewed by others as a success for a range of factors from professional to personal. But even now, if a man and a woman who happened to be parents were at a cocktail party together, the guy would most likely be asked about his job, and the woman would most likely be asked about her kids. Even if she's an executive. Even if he's a dad of three who works part-time.

Do you see how there's already an uphill climb to reach "involved dad" status as a natural state of being where people don't assume it's the woman who defaults to being a primary caregiver? Why can't we assume there's a strong possibility that the mom works and the dad stays at home?

According to Pew Research, "17% of all stay-at-home parents in 2016 were fathers, up from 10% in 1989." So sure, it's not likely the dad is staying home, but it's trending in the right direction! In fact there are national stay-at-home dad organizations and even a Dad 2.0 blogger conference. (I've gone several times and met dads of all kinds from around the country and the world. It's amazing.)

It's not as unusual as it once was to say, "I'm a dad and I like to get involved with my kids."

But ...

Sometimes it feels, despite all the progress, like we could easily slip back into a *Downton Abbey*-style approach where the men retire to smoke a cigar after dinner and the women are left to rear the children. (OK, they had, like, 14 nannies in that show but still.) For every celebrity dad taking selfies with his kids on a daddy/daughter date, there are politicians voting against paternal leave, female CEOs getting sexist questions about how they could possibly "give up their family" to pursue a career and dads left and right being celebrated for burning the midnight oil to help make an extra buck without anyone asking, "Hey, what about your baby?"

(Quick sidebar: I'm not knocking any dad who is trying to provide for his family and, as a result, sometimes has to push himself hard for a promotion or a bonus. It's not the short spurts, which can be expected. It's the marathon with tunnel vision where you forget why you're earning money in the first place.)

In the alternative world where 50/50 child-raising duties are assumed, men would start getting more questions about how they are succeeding as parents, not just how they are succeeding as professionals. I bet in that world, men would more often feel a sense of pride and accomplishment as a result of those frequent trips to the playground or museum. Guys aren't shy about wanting to be awesome at what we do; it's just that "what we do" isn't usually defined by outsiders as "being a dad."

If he could get *that* kind of equality, he could still love his career, but when someone asks questions related to his happiness and purpose in life, his instincts would be to talk about his family because that's where he feels the most fulfilled.

It's a mistake to assume your partner is predicting fatherhood will change his life in the same way you predict motherhood will change yours.

Beyond the logistics, he hasn't put nearly as much thought into it as you have. He knows life is going to be different, but chances are he's more worried about what's being taken away than what's being added.

That's not to say that you assumed motherhood would be a never-ending pleasure full of kisses and lavender and giggles. You've had girlfriends and aunts and coworkers give you the real scoop and open your eyes. Especially your loudmouth, oversharing aunt who talks about childbirth like it's a scene from *The Walking Dead*.

They probably followed up that real talk, however, with tales of how they loved seeing their baby smile for the first time, or they went on and on about how their baby is the smartest baby in daycare. (Every parent thinks their kid is the smartest baby in daycare. They're wrong, of course. Because mine are.)

I'm here to say that guys aren't getting the same scoop as women.

I did a straw poll and asked dozens of other dads across the country the following question:

"Before you became a dad, what did friends/family tell you about fatherhood?"

The most popular answer was, "Fatherhood would mostly be tough."

Second most popular? "No one talked to me about being a dad."

Can you imagine that, moms? NO ONE talked to them about what to expect.

When my wife found out that she was pregnant with our oldest, people emerged like pigeons gobbling up discarded bread at the park for the chance to talk about childbirth. They would toss out morsels about their childbirths and what she should know and what she should buy.

They also said plenty of terribly inappropriate things, but that's another topic. Let's just say, "Hey, any day now, eh?" is never an appropriate remark to make to a pregnant woman. Especially to one who is only seven months pregnant.

One time, a Walmart cashier saw my very pregnant wife come down her checkout lane and said, "I hope you don't go into labor right now because if you do, the store policy is that I have to help clean it up."

Which is a great reminder that A) Walmart has a lot of in-store births and B) If you hear "clean up in aisle 8," don't go look. That's placenta.

For the most part, though, people flooded her with attention, stories and support. It was heartwarming, even if it was also confusing to know what to trust.

Meanwhile, guys aren't being talked to about expectations, and the attention they do get is flippant drivel like, "Guess you better clear out the man cave!" because people don't know how to talk to dads about fatherhood.

When we found out we were having twin girls, I had strangers tell me, "Uh oh, better watch out for boys when they get older!" and I'm thinking, "WTF? Did you just warn me about holding off teen boys from sleeping with my yet-to-be-born daughters?"

For those expectant dads in my poll who said people *did* talk to them about what to expect, the majority told me they heard how tough it would be compared to the (much) smaller segment that heard how amazing fatherhood could be.

Dads are told about diaper changes. And rising expenses. And sleepless nights. And lack of time and freedom.

"I think I had this idealized vision of what being a parent was like. People who I did speak to painted a much gloomier picture of how it would be than the reality," one dad, Ross, said.

It's like you and your partner are about to enter the same skyscraper but you're being let off at different floors.

As comedian Jim Gaffigan says:

> Every night before I get my one hour of sleep, I have the same thought: "Well, that's a wrap on another day of acting like I know what I'm doing." I wish I were exaggerating, but I'm not. Most of the time, I feel entirely unqualified to be a parent. I call these times being awake.

I can't even keep count of how many nonsense things perfect strangers have told my wife. People feel entitled to opinions simply because the baby is in their presence. It was even worse when she was pregnant.

"My ass was wide like that too! I bet you're having a boy as well," some crazy lady once said to her.

I don't get nearly that many looks or comments. As a dad, the assumption is more often than not that it's just nice I'm helping at all. Like, it's a bonus instead of essential so they don't want to judge lest I say, "Screw it! I don't need this criticism! I'm a man!" and leave my son in the Kohl's parking lot. I've wanted to leave my son in a parking lot for many reasons but not because of that.

(If you're picking up on my distaste for the unsolicited opinions of strangers about child rearing, you are discerning correctly. I've awarded you 500 bonus points.)

You need to soak in the following popular sentiment because it's a stereotype your soon-to-be involved husband will face regularly:

Moms parent. Dads babysit.

In the more than six years that I've been a dad, I've heard variations of that theme again and again, and it always makes me either chuckle or shake my head.

I get some equivocation of "How wonderful you're involved as a father, you poor, helpless chap" most often when we're on a family vacation, as that's when parenting always gets cranked up a few levels; i.e., you're even more visible doing dad stuff.

Now sure, the three-kids-three-and-under thing we had going on for some time meant a lot of people wondered how my wife and I accomplished just about anything. The answer: Patience, a lot of planning and snacks. I don't care who you are — if someone puts fruit snacks in front of you, you're going to be happier. Fact.

But there's another set of comments I've heard a lot when we do our regular trips to the New Jersey coastline, especially on walks by the beach. These comments reinforce the idea that even now, many people assume dads aren't involved and that it's a blessing if they are, which then creates a cycle of guys thinking they don't need to be involved because it's not expected.

A typical scene that has often garnered the attention of strangers when we're on vacation is when I've taken all three kids on a walk in our double stroller. With the warm sea air brushing our faces and the comforting low rumble of stroller wheels rolling over boardwalk planks reverberating in our ears, it's a lovely way to spend an hour or so.

Just a dad out with his three kids on vacation.

Admittedly, when most of the boardwalk is filled with runners, bikers and single-baby strollers, we stand out. I'd probably do a double-take too, and it never gets old to have people say your kids are cute. That's the kind of friendly gesture that helps balance out those moments when they aren't being so cute. I'm not a murderer, but my babies have essentially accused me of as much when I've put them in their car seats. Death by safety buckle! It's the silent killer.

So, you've got the scene in your head: a dad pushing his kids down the boardwalk. You'd think people had never seen a dad spending time alone with his own children out in public.

A sample of what I was told on just *one* trip:

"God, give you strength."

"I remember those days. Giving the wife a break, eh?"

"Best of luck."

"Oh wow."

"Good for you."

"Wow ... need another one?"

All comments made with good intentions, all said with a smile, all meant to be complementary.

Switch around the gender, though, and it's a different sentiment entirely. Imagine it's my wife walking with the kids. How many times do you think she would hear, "Giving the dad a break, eh?" or "Good for you" about her ability to be out with the kids on her own.

How many times do you think *you'd* hear that?

I'm taking a good guess your partner will.

There are definitely times when I go out of my way to take all the kids out of the house so my wife can have some time alone without someone pulling on her leg, but she does the same for me. We approach it as co-parenting. Together. They are *our* kids. I rely on my wife a tremendous amount and I'm so thankful to have her with me to tackle the crazy world of parenting (her patience is second only to her kindness for unbelievable traits), but she also relies on me. It's never exactly the same, but we don't approach it as a "I did this so you have to do that" quid pro quo kind of deal.

Passersby wouldn't know how much we try to share parenting. They just see a dad out with his kids. For example, one time when the kids and I were at a department store checkout after my wife left early to go get the car, the cashier commented how brave I was for shopping alone with the kids. I asked my wife if she'd ever gotten that kind of comment — nope!

Who's to blame for seeing a guy out with his kids and assuming he's taking a risk by watching all his kids at once or that the only reason he's doing it is to provide a brief respite for the mom? No one in particular. Pop culture says dads can't handle babies. History says dads aren't as involved as moms. I get it! Until recently, we didn't hear much about dads being involved parents.

Those kinds of comments show that we have a long way to go.

We ought to assume that dads can and will be involved parents.

Guys simply haven't been told their whole lives that, if they become fathers, they will be expected to take the baby to the grocery store alone, change diapers at 4 a.m., do the daycare drop off and put family in front of career. We're just not there yet.

That means it will likely be harder for your partner to *assume* he's meant for that role unless he's been fortunate enough to have had great role models within his family or friend group.

This makes for a great opportunity for both of you!

I find more and more dads want to be viewed as essential personnel when it comes to parenting. Not because they want credit like a co-worker craving attention from a boss on a work project, not because of some ego boost (because that assumes they are doing something extra special), but because once everyone starts assuming dads should be as involved as moms, the standard increases for all fathers. When that happens, people will have less tolerance for guys who think it's the mom's job to raise their kids.

I'm talking about a culture shift and a needed one, at that.

The way that happens is by one dad at a time taking care of his kids at home, in public, at the beach and everywhere in-between the same way that moms are expected to.

Dads don't babysit, as the hugely popular National At-Home Dads Network T-shirt says. They parent.

I can't wait until that becomes ridiculously obvious to state. I can't wait until your partner thinks likewise.

Let's talk more about how we can make that happen for your family.

2

Don't hope for involved fatherhood. Expect it.

Raise the expectations. Your partner is capable of more.

For a lot of guys, Dwayne "The Rock" Johnson is the epitome of manliness. In one of the *Fast & Furious* sequels (Yes, I've seen every single one. Don't @ me.), he busts out of an arm cast by flexing his forearm. He gets all the ladies on screen. He even wrestled a shark and won.*

 * *Not true, but for half a second, you thought, "Huh."*

He's also extremely funny. Some of my favorite roles of his are comedies like *Central Intelligence*, and let's not even get started on how great he is in *Moana*.

What your partner might not know, though, is that by all appearances, The Rock is an amazing father. Also, despite being one of the biggest and busiest celebrities in the world, he's an advocate for sharing parenting duties. One example on his Instagram account, which has, uh ... 133 million(!) followers, is a post showing him feeding his girlfriend while she breastfeeds their baby, Tiana.

"Mama @laurenhashianofficial has her hands full nursing/feeding Baby Tia, so I'm feedin' mama her dinner. My pleasure," he wrote.

Does it get any manlier than that?

Now, I'll caveat all of this and any other celebrity reference you'll see in this book by saying that you never know what's going on behind closed doors. That goes for all of us. But I think it would be hard to fake that kind of involvement. There's a genuine appreciation for what his girlfriend is trying to accomplish and for how he can be involved.

This is a dude who took on the San Andreas Fault and won, and he's making sure his partner gets what she needs to be a supported mother.

Hell yes.

As a society that so heavily relies on celebrities to act as our North Star for feeling and behaving, how much better off would we be if we saw more men with *that* kind of influence showing humility and valuing fatherhood? Guys around the world need to see this type of thing more often.

Unfortunately, that world isn't here yet.

Thanks to social media, it's certainly more accessible, but it will take a few decades for all of this to soak in and make a generational impact. You need thousands of posts, stories and videos of high-profile men being involved fathers, coupled with everyday examples and role models, for a generation of guys to see that this is the way it needs to be.

I'd like to stop here and say that there is an amazing army of moms out there who are doing a fantastic job rocking this parenting thing alone. And there are also a lot of moms who are supported by close friends and family who live nearby and can offer her the respite of a couple of hours "kid free."

(If you haven't already, you'll learn how just going to Target by yourself can be orgasmic. My wife basically considers it dating herself if she gets to go to Target alone. Even better when she can grab a tea from the Starbucks inside.)

Family and friends are great. Essential, even. Having them around can make the difference between keeping your sanity and losing your shit some days.

But I think we can all agree that it's not the same as having an equal partner around. Every day. Every hour. Not just someone who is present, but someone who is *present*.

With this sort of partner, there's no need to ask "If it's OK with you, could you..." There's no need to stop and think, "Well, I already asked him to change a diaper today ..." because you're 100% in this thing together.

So what do you do, new mom?

You're not The Rock, I presume. Although if you are, hey! *You're wellcccoommmeeee.*

You're reading this because you're in this whole parenting craziness with a partner, and you're looking for ways to make sure he's involved, he's confident, and he's right there with you. You don't have time for Dwayne Johnson to post another adorable photo. You need your husband to step up *now*.

I call the kind of guy you need an "E–I–E–O" dad.

Is your partner an "E-I-E-O" Dad?

First off, apologies for the "Old Macdonald" reference. I hear a lot of toddler songs. I used to listen to Radiohead and the Fugees. Now I only listen to songs that are all choruses with no stanzas. Also, dads get a hard pass on all bad puns. Forever.

So, how do you know if your partner is what I call an Equally-Involved, Equal Opportunity (E-I-E-I-O) Dad, the kind of guy that sees parenting as a mutually beneficial partnership?

Take this quiz about what your partner might do/has done in the following situations:

1. You need to make a baby registry. Does he:

- A) Grab the scanning gun — he's ready! The two of you divided up the list so that you didn't have to research everything, and he's anxious to get started.
- B) Put in his two cents on car seats and cribs but mostly lets you decide on the specifics because that's "not really my thing" and he doesn't want to suggest the wrong idea. Whatever shows up at your house is fine.
- C) Roll his eyes when you talk about it. He doesn't see what the big deal is about a baby shower. It's fine that you're having one, but that's your thing, not his.
- D) Start worrying that you are going to take away his man cave and fill it up with baby toys. What's next, a MINIVAN?

2. The baby just dropped a diaper bomb so hard that Febreze stock instantly spiked 14%. Meanwhile, you're up to your ears in preparing dinner. Your partner:

- A) Changes the diaper without you asking. Who cares whose turn it is?
- B) Waits to see if you'll change it, then begrudgingly grabs a new diaper because he knows it's his turn.
- C) Says "Wow, that diaper reeks!" in a passive-aggressive tone and goes on with his business after making a big deal out of the last time he changed a diaper.

17

- D) Is not in the same room as you. He's in the man cave waiting for dinner to be ready. He went to work today. That's his contribution.

3. It's time for the 6-month checkup!

- A) Great! He'll meet you at the doctor. He's got a few questions ready to go.
- B) He asks how it went after you text him that you're leaving the appointment.
- C) After you mention the baby seems fine, he brushes off your update from the doctor and changes the subject.
- D) You've long since stopped trying to keep him in the loop with what's going on. He didn't go to any of your OB-GYN appointments, after all, and let's not even start on what happened that time you asked him to pick up tampons at the store.

4. You aren't feeling great and could really use a Saturday to yourself. When you bring up the possibility of him taking your daughter for the day, he ...

- A) Says no problem and whisks her away for some daddy-daughter time. His diaper bag is always at the ready, and he's no stranger to being out alone with her.
- B) Offers to take her out for a long stroller ride so you can lie down for an hour. He wants to help but also gets anxious thinking of taking her all day without backup. It's a small break, at least.
- C) Doesn't get the hint until it's clear you're bedridden. He calls his mom to come watch her granddaughter. Great.

Now your mother-in-law is here, and you feel like she's probably judging you for slacking off. At least he somewhat tried.

- D) Complains that he already worked all week and he just wants one day to himself. You fight about it but you don't want to make a big deal, so you let him go out with his friends. Maybe you can power through it.

5. If you showed up at his job with the baby, would his coworkers...

- A) Say "Finally! We've been dying to meet this bundle of joy. He's all your husband/boyfriend talks about!"
- B) Smile and nod as they put two and two together that you must have had the baby. He did mention a few times at work that you were expecting.
- C) Say, "Oh, are you babysitting a little niece or nephew today?"
- D) Hahahaha — he would never let you bring the baby near his work.

6. You're at a party together and someone notices you brought your baby (Because how else are you both at a party?) and asks how big she was at birth.

- A) He jumps in and says "7 pounds 12 ounces" right away and then talks about the delivery, raving about what a rock star you are. Would you like to see photos? He's filled up his entire iPhone with them.
- B) He defers to you, knowing she weighed somewhere between 2 and 28 pounds, but he has a smile on his face

because he does enjoy talking about his daughter and takes pride in being a dad.

- C) He mentally checks out. Why are people so obsessed with how much the baby weighed? He loves you and his daughter, but outside of the house, he'd rather talk about anything else.
- D) He's been huddled around the grill for the past hour in his "safe zone," away from all the baby talk so he can get a break, which is really rich coming from him.

7. The baby has a fever and you're not home ...

- A) No problem. He knows where the baby Tylenol is and how to use the thermometer, and he's no stranger to the nurse hotline. Taking the baby to urgent care wouldn't be a big ordeal for him.
- B) He texts you regular updates and to see how much longer you'll be. He'd rather not take her to the doctor himself, but he will if he has to because he wants your baby to get better soon. Generally, though, the doctor is "your thing."
- C) He keeps saying, "She's fine. It's not a big deal," and you're wondering if that's really the case or if he's even checked the baby's temperature lately. You feel a little uneasy about not being there.
- D) This would never be the case. You're not leaving the baby with your partner unless everything is ideal. He's just not the nurturing type.

How did your dude do?

Mostly A's: You've got one hell of an E-I-E-O Dad there. He's already showing strong commitment! If he's that enthusiastic about being involved now, you have a great shot at having a strong parenting partnership. Keep it up!

Mostly A's and B's: A fantastic start. He's got some hesitancy, maybe because he's not quite sure what to do or when he should step in and take more ownership. The more you talk to him about what would be helpful, the better. He wants to do more! He just needs some guidance. You should feel optimistic.

Mostly B's, C's and D's: Some days, he seems super involved. Other days, he gives you the impression that parenting is more annoying than anything. Let's figure out what's really going on here. There's a possibility that your partner is erecting emotional walls so that he doesn't have to reveal his insecurity. It's no small step to go from just another guy to a father.

Mostly D's: Every step of the way, he seems to do the opposite of what you'd want from the father of your child. Please don't sit and hope that one day he'll flip the proverbial switch and magically become the partner you need him to be. It will take real work born out of good communication for him to see what you need and how rewarding parenting can be, if he would just give it a chance.

How do you feel about the results? You should now have an idea of where your partner falls on the involvement scale.

What kind of ownership does it feel like he's taking?

We need to let the answers to these questions soak in and move on to figuring out how to work through and eventually communicate your expectations.

Here's the deal: I often get the sense that, even though she is in a happy, committed relationship with a guy who ought to be taking a big part of the responsibility, some moms still feel as though they'll be doing it alone.

It's as if they drank the pop culture Kool-Aid too. They

assume that since their husband never seems interested in other people's kids, it's going to be all on her once their own baby arrives.

These women have heard too many stories from friends about how so-and-so's husband won't lift a finger to help. They've read countless Facebook posts about exasperated, exhausted moms pleading for a nap, even though a perfectly able husband must be nearby. They've become desensitized by hearing, yet again, that a girlfriend's partner is "going out with the guys" instead of helping to prepare for their baby's birthday party.

Those stories circulate for a reason. They're based on real experiences, and I bet you've seen a few first-hand.

Men are really blowing it in these cases, and they're making us all look bad.

Hey, I have definitely been guilty of taking a step back instead of jumping in to help, and early on as a dad, I took credit too easily for responsibilities that were shared. So shame on me, too.

Thankfully, I've learned.

Men need to take the dad role seriously. Too often, we treat it like a hobby.

(*Let's make an agreement now that I'm not saying ALL men underperform as dads, nor that if you waved a magic wand and changed societal roles, ALL guys would step up. Some are just lazy or selfish. What we do know is that there's room to help those who want to do more!*)

You hear about new dads who are asked to do the bare minimum but then have the audacity to ask if the bar can be lowered. To make matters worse, when they do achieve that low bar of parental involvement, they brag about it, asking for a pat on the back.

It's not like you had the option. You are neck deep in it no matter what.

You never hear men saying to each other, "You know what? My wife just sits on her butt all day while I'm getting our son fed, clothed, bathed and burped. She always says she already *has* a full-time job and that she's too tired to take care of the baby."

Number one, that would be an insane conversation. Number two, you never hear that because women are so, so, *so* much better at embracing motherhood, even if they're also freaked out by it.

Moms will work full-time and pump in a dirty bathroom if that's the only option, because that's what needs to be done.

Moms will juggle a part-time, at-home job and keep the entire house going while looking up organic baby food recipes, because that's what needs to be done.

When the baby comes, we look to moms to check things off the list.

Believe me, I appreciate the irony that scores of dudes who spend endless hours playing a video game called "Call of Duty" won't answer the call of duty for someone they literally created with their penises.

You deserve better.

As a mom, it's not your responsibility to get the dad motivated, like some overzealous trainer trying to get a New Year's resolution gym member to show up and hit the elliptical on a Monday in March.

Let me make that clear: In the end, the guy needs to embrace the role.

It's not on you to have to beg him to help when the baby gets up in the night. It's not on you to provide enough energy and enthusiasm for the both of you.

He's an adult. He was adult enough to jump your bones. He's adult enough to change a diaper.

But, if we're talking about ways to nudge your husband closer to that "E-I-E-O" status, I believe you have to make your expectations crystal clear.

Expectations set the stage for involved fatherhood.

From the start (or starting today, if you've already got a baby in tow), *your expectation needs to be that he will be an involved dad.*

No less.

Let's repeat this because it's crucial:

Your expectation as a mom needs to be that your partner *will* be an involved father.

How does that work?

Well, it starts with how you speak to him. In your conversations, it's not a "Well, maybe you can help at night sometimes?" Instead, try "How do you want to split up late night diaper changes?"

My wife is many wonderful things, and, to be candid, I'm even close to the father I am because she makes it easier for me. She gives me pep talks. She cuts me slack, especially when I've struggled with balancing work stress with parenting stress. She always makes me feel like I'm a better parent.

What was the secret ingredient? **She never assumed I would coast along while she took care of our baby.** She let me know when all the doctor appointments were, she had me involved when it came to childcare decisions, we discussed parenting methods and much more. Even if I had wanted to let my responsibilities slide, it wouldn't have happened because **she**

had made her expectations clear: She would not be doing this by herself. It wouldn't even be an 80/20 situation. We were a parenting partnership from day one because my wife would settle for no less.

That made it all the more easy for me to deliver on what she needed, and in return, it made me feel more fulfilled as a dad because I had *earned* it. If I was out with my son by myself, I could freely talk about anything from his last doctor check-up to his growth to what it took to soothe him in the middle of the night. I earned that by participating, and that started with Sara's expectation that I'd do no less than be fully involved. The goal is to create a culture in which you are both taking full responsibility for the life that you equally created.

You know that saying about wealthy kids, "They were born on third base and think they hit a triple"?

Don't let your husband take advantage of you doing all the work of raising your kid and then reap the benefit of everyone thinking that he's an involved father.

Expect the best from your partner. Expect what you deserve.

I'm very sure no one is expecting you to be an uninvolved mom. No one assumes they'll need to *ask* you to be nurturing and caring. Pediatricians are going to guess that you're the one who knows everything about your kid's health history, even if your partner is standing right there. Hell, I've had a nurse or two act like I didn't even exist and speak directly to my wife about our baby, even though I had been at the appointment and paying attention the whole time.

Expectations matter.

A funny thing might happen if you start making those same assumptions and start setting those same expectations.

He might just meet them.

You might feel like you don't know what you're doing and that everyone expects the world from you. Who wouldn't? You're expected to be a great mom. And sexy at all times. And attend every fucking LuLaRoe party your friends have.

Your partner also feels like he doesn't know what he's doing and won't come into parenting having spent much time, if any, thinking about his role as a father. That has an impact. I know many dads who had never held a baby until the nurse handed them their own, which is kind of ridiculous if you think about it; that's like someone never having driven a car and then the dealer hands over the keys to a Ferrari and says, "Have fun! See ya!"

This creates a sweet opportunity for you, mom.

He's a clean slate! And he wants to be good at this. Guys really, really, *really* hate to not be good at things. The thought of looking like an idiot while they watch you look like a natural makes them feel like they shouldn't try at all, because at least then no one will see right through them. That is ass-backward thinking, short-sighted and dumb, yes. Mostly, though, it's the age-old problem of guys not talking about what they're feeling.

If you assume that he will be an uninvolved dad and push him to the margins of conversations about how to take care of your kid, he will naturally feel like you have the same doubts he does about his capabilities. If you assume he's going to be amazing, he'll start out feeling more confident, and a confident dad is a dad who embraces his responsibility.

If you haven't already, start clearly communicating what needs to be done. Not in a sassy, "it's your baby, too!" way that will make him feel defensive. Instead, take the approach that you're in this together. Let him know that you need to know that he sees it as a partnership too, and "here are a few things I'd like you to do so that I can feel less overwhelmed." If he tries a few and maybe one or two don't work out, that's not a failure! He's trying, and maybe you'll discover that he has a method that, while possibly different from yours, works just as well. Remind him that you're figuring this all out too.

Raised expectations. Improved outcome. And a dad who's earned it.

3

Emotional wreck for two, please.

Tears will flow out of nowhere.

Have you ever seen your partner cry?
    You might be replaying a stereotypical joke in your head right
now:

- "Only when we run out of beer!"
- "Only when his team loses in the playoffs!"
- "Only when the 'Undercover Boss' reveals themselves and
  then hands out scholarships and money to his surprised
  employees at the end of the episode!"

OK, that last one was about me, but you get the point. We jump
to a snarky joke because the thought of an adult male crying
seems like a joke.
    It's no wonder. We're already not as prone to crying in the
first place, and, as boys, we don't see many examples of grown
men crying, unless it's used for comedic effect when he spills

his beer or his team loses the big championship. Crying isn't the only emotional outburst that matters, but it is the one that we most often associate with being sensitive.

If your husband is in the midst of a tear drought, fatherhood will end it.

As you are adjusting your expectations for what your partner is both capable of and should achieve, I want to make you aware that he's most likely going through "The Change."

Not that change. He's not getting hot flashes.

I'm talking about the change that happens when a guy who, up to this point, has spent his waking hours thinking about a promotion at work or a fantasy football waiver wire claim but will now, seemingly without warning, find his thoughts crowded with "What if's" and "Will my baby be OK?"

Becoming a dad, like I imagine it is for moms, supercharges your emotions. In particular, it makes guys constantly think about their livelihood (because now they have a legacy, as well as much more to lose if something happens to them). It makes them look at you in a whole new way (my love for my wife has skyrocketed as a result of watching her as a mother), and it causes dads to get much more in touch with their emotions.

He'll hear songs on the radio that remind him of your baby and he'll tear up. Or your baby grows a little and he'll get misty-eyed, thinking about how the baby used to fit on his chest. Or he'll get terrified out of nowhere wondering how he'd ever survive if something bad happened to her. Guys are so used to operating independently, without much regard to how we impact others (just look at the workplace), but now there's a baby who blows up that whole mindset.

I slowly realized how much of every action I took as a new dad was in response to what was best for my kids and less and less about what was best for me.

One example: Drinking soda (Or pop, if you want to be correct about it! #westernPArepresent): I was already going to cut down on sugar, but I doubled down on it by cutting out soda completely, because I didn't want my kids to see me drinking it and wonder why I wouldn't let them have any. My actions were motivated by how my choice impacted them. I couldn't make a decision about what to eat in a vacuum; I had to consider what I wanted my kids to think.

And hell, that's just a 50-grams-of-sugar decision. The stakes are usually much higher.

Fatherhood inspires me to think of all kinds of life-and-death shit.

What would happen if our house caught on fire? I know for certain that I would die from smoke inhalation if that's what it took to get to my kid.

One morning when my son was three or four, he told us that he had a nightmare. Most of his nightmares were tame. In this one? He dreamt that the house was burning and he was crouched down in his room waiting for mommy or daddy to save him, but we never came.

Yes, I know. I KNOW.

What he doesn't know is that I would pull down a burning door with my bare hands if that's what it took. *That's* how fatherhood changes guys. You begin to funnel all of that untapped protection-and-providing instinct into your love for one beautiful baby.

Pre-dad, outside of my career, I wasn't exactly in tearing-down-doors mode about much of anything. Most single guys in their 20s aren't. We're way into video games or fantasy sports or climbing the corporate ladder. For the most part, we're not doing a lot of "How can I take care of and nurture others around me?"

Becoming a dad meant that what now kept me up at night was the thought of anything happening to my kids.

If you haven't noticed already, part of the overall theme here is that fatherhood is going to transform your husband.

This might be one of the most visible changes because, perhaps for the first time, he'll start wearing his emotions on his sleeve. *(That is, unless he's one of those jacked dudes who never wears sleeves because he wants everyone to see what $472 a month in protein shakes got him. In that case, he wears his emotions on his tank top. Also, if you want an idea of what happens in men's locker rooms, it's mostly guys mixing protein shakes, talking about business and sports and flexing in the mirror.)*

That's what having a baby will do to you — it brings out deep emotions. And weird fluids because babies are messy but, yes, emotions too. Anxiety. Sadness. Terror.

Which sounds like a bad sequel to Pixar's *Inside Out*.

Babies make you grow such deep freaking joy that you show complete strangers a photo of your baby half-smiling because you can't NOT do that.

Many dad friends of mine confessed that they are *much more* emotional now than they ever were. And that can be a hard thing for dudes to process. Not because of some antiquated "Me man, me don't cry" B.S., but because we literally don't understand what's happening to us. The last time we were such an emotional wreck, we were busy growing two inches overnight, having hair sprout in weird places and spending each day being terrified of girls.

Here's the thing. This sensitive side, which is unveiled by fatherhood? It's actually a powerful motivator for becoming a more involved dad. It's like a hidden secret weapon, and it can make all the difference when it comes to your partner's willingness to be a *partner*. So, how do you help him embrace it?

What goes a long way for a new dad is giving him space to work through this.

If a guy feels like his partner is just going to make fun of him for showing a more sensitive side, he'll hide it like a turtle retreating into it's shell. Wouldn't you do likewise? Instead, whatever a partner can do to show support is crucial, not unlike what moms expect on their end.

An involved dad is one who is heavily emotionally invested.

That means we have to open up. That means we can't shy away from feeling vulnerable, maybe for the first time. That means we are confused on the daily about our emotional state when we were so used to being "Cool, I guess," and knowing you appreciate that we aren't hiding it.

This is weird for us. Trust me, I know.

How I found myself weeping over a children's book:

When my son was our one-and-only, we had a nightly ritual.

Usually, it didn't involve me weeping and clutching his hand. But on this night, it did.

My son was two years old, and I would read and rock him to sleep every night. It's a ritual that used to take more than an hour, as my son equated sleep to giving up on the day, and he's no quitter. Except when it comes to listening. He quits listening all the time.

Night after night, I would sit down in a blue-padded rocking chair and read whatever book my son handed me.

Goodnight Moon? Sure. *A to Z Animals*? A for awesome. *The*

Cat in the Hat? How about that? He had an entire bookshelf full of options.

One night, with a sleepy smile on his face, he handed me a book, said "Up?" and held out his outstretched arms just like he always would. He settled in on my lap, a lap that used to hold him easily, but one that, with each passing month, felt more like a clown car.

That's when I realized what book he handed me.

It was that classic, tear-jerking *Love You Forever* book.

NOOOO! That book is the cry factory!

It's what you read if you want your face to look like a living reenactment of the canoe scene from *The Notebook*!

So do you remember Robert Munsch's *Love You Forever?* Of course you do. He's sold 15 million copies, or about 14,999,999 more copies than your friend has sold of her e-book about the incredible shrinking power of body wraps.

The familiar light blue cover of *Love You Forever* is enough to get your waterworks going; an artist's drawing of a little boy covered in toilet paper and memories, tugging at your heartstrings before you even turn the first page because your kids are basically all 30 years old now and where did the time go and my God how did they get so big so fast?

Here's what some parents don't know, though: This book is even sadder than you thought in the most real and worst way possible.

The author came up with the story idea after he and his wife had two stillborn babies, a devastating experience to say the least.

"The song (in the book) was my song to my dead babies," Munsch wrote on his website.

ARE YOU KIDDING ME?

I don't even know how to process something so heart-wrenching. For those of you who have dealt with this loss, my heart goes out to you. There's nothing anyone could say that could heal that kind of hurt.

I find it incredible that this dad was able to channel his grief and write a beloved book out of such tragic experiences.

Now that you know the back story, try reading that book to your kid. I double-dog dare you. I can tell you right now, it will not go well. Parenting is already fraught with random, emotional zings that come out of nowhere, causing innocent quiet moments to morph you into a pile of misty-eyed, babbling "Remember when" mush. I didn't need a book to provide a 5-Hour Energy for my inner emotional wreck to turn on the faucet.

But when your son wants you to read a book, you read that book. So I began to read. I gingerly turned to the first page, waiting for the emotional roller coaster like a movie heroine waits in the fetal position for the chainsaw murderer to arrive.

I began to read as my son pressed his blonde hair into my shoulder. When I first earnestly started reading to him, months prior to that point, he would curiously stare at the pages. He couldn't read letters yet and mostly just liked to look at the visuals. By this point, though, he knew the entire alphabet and followed along with the storyline.

The first time I came across the *Love You Forever* main stanza, I made it through with dry eyes. Whew.

I love you forever / I'll like you for always / As long as I'm living / My baby you'll be.

Punch me right in the feels, Munsch! What's next, a chapter

about how we're all just marching toward inevitable death and childhood is a mere footnote?

As the boy in the book advances in age and his mother quietly sings him the same haunting tune, I, in turn, quietly started shedding tears.

By the time the boy in the book becomes a teenager, I was actively weeping. I mean, tears streaming down my face like they were trying to escape from prison, and not a white collar prison or an *Orange Is the New Black* prison but, like, *prison-prison*.

When did my son get so big? Did he always take up my entire lap? Would he one day not want to hang out with his dad? Is he graduating high school right this very second?

And then, as I finished the book, I sang the stanza to my son one more time, barely getting through it in the dimly lit room as my voice cracked.

My son saw all of this. He soaked it in, literally, and, as I told him it was time to go to sleep, he turned on his side, grabbed my left hand and pulled it very tightly across his chest as we rocked and rocked.

He eventually fell asleep, but when I put him in his crib, he woke up just a little bit and grabbed my hand again, pulling it under him like a security blanket and refusing to let go.

Maybe it was his way of saying he'll love me forever, too.

That, moms, is what I'm talking about; an emotional out-pouring that I never saw coming. It was one night. One book. And yet that's the kind of thing that helped power me through the tougher moments on the days when it would have been so tempting to phone it in. Tapping into that kind of powerful emotion can be a big difference maker, so the more your partner gets the chance to do that, the better. Dads are just catching up to where moms have been for months.

Finding the right balance.

No doubt, you've been feeling pretty heavy emotions lately. Whether you're pregnant now, are postpartum, or shit, WHEN-EVER, you've been dealing with some turbulent emotional stuff for some time now.

The thought of your partner maybe *just now* getting on the rollercoaster with you might make you want to punch him.

Like, "Dude, where were you before?"

He's been there, just maybe not exactly on the ride. More like you were both in the same Pregnancy Land Amusement Park, but you were on the Double-Helix 100-mph rollercoaster and he was on the Teacups.

It can take the actual arrival of the baby to get him buckled in next to you on the emotional rollercoaster of parenting. Odds are, he's not handling it as well as you are, and those same odds are that he's not telling you how he's feeling. What would help?

It would be reassuring for him to know that you're going through the same thing and that you're just figuring it out as you go as well. He might be thinking he'll sound like an idiot if he tells you that he gets afraid of the baby getting hurt. Or that he gets misty-eyed thinking of how happy he is when he rocks her at night. Or that he's worried he won't be able to financially support the family like he always thought he would. Or that he is screwing up all the time and you're so awesome at being a mom (even if you don't feel that way!), and he's just freaking stressed *out*.

Tonight, after one of you puts the baby down, grab his hand. Give him a kiss on the cheek.

Say, "This has been crazy, hasn't it? I don't know if you're as freaked out as I am, but I love that you _____," and let him know some quirky, little thing he does for the baby that you've secretly admired. He should be doing this as well. Dads need to remind moms that they are appreciated and noticed. The truth is that you both deserve to take a moment and appreciate the insanity of what you're trying to do. It makes a big difference if you'll take that moment together, hand in hand, every chance you get.

4

Gratitude is not optional.

He can't say he's involved but then ignore your needs.

Imagine two scenarios.

In one, both you and your partner are pushing through each day. You're both super involved, and your baby is as nurtured and loved as anyone can wish for at any given moment, but it's draining the two of you faster than a bank account after a Target run. You're both emotionally depleted, as you're spending all of your positive energy keeping the baby happy. He gets his part done. You do yours. There's no love lost. But there's no love nourished. You're just kinda working through the to-do list, day by day by day.

In another scenario, you're both super involved, but you send a quick "thank you" text to your partner after he intuitively steps in when the baby had been crying for hours and he knew you were at your breaking point. He sends a smiley emoji back, glad to know you noticed that he was trying to take care of both of you. Later, he gives you a long hug and says he appreciates that you got up last night (when it wasn't technically "your turn") to take care of a feeding, knowing he needed to get up extra early for work that morning.

And so back and forth you go, never doing anything because you *expect* a thank you or an "attaboy/girl," but because you are reciprocating kindness. I don't know about you, but if I'm already going to do something I wouldn't usually want to do, it's sure a welcome gesture when my partner recognizes the situation and takes the time to be grateful.

With this approach, both of you are receiving so much more without exerting that much more energy (because ain't nobody got extra energy right now). He's gaining confidence that he can handle being a dad because the person he loves and respects the most is noticing what he's doing, and you're feeling appreciated by a more active and loving partner.

I love doing things for my wife. I don't do it to suck up. Really, it might just be my love language. You've heard about those, I bet — the different ways people show someone they love them and how they want to receive love in return. Mine has always been acts of service. My wife knows that, so she's fantastic at acknowledging when I try to do something for her. She knows that serving her is my way of expressing my love for her. Especially when I'd empty the Diaper Genie. That was expressing a lot of love.

Maybe your partner has a different way of expressing how he loves you, which might mean that he isn't diving into doing the little things because he's feeling like he's already supporting you by giving you encouragement or rubbing your shoulders or researching daycares. If that works for you, let him know. But if that's not enough, you need to let him know that as well. Otherwise, you'll be building resentment, and he'll be confused as to why you never seem happy with his efforts.

Whichever way you like to show your appreciation, make gratitude a non-negotiable. You have to be thankful for what each of you brings to the table! How miserable would it be to raise a kid if we all felt like we're just punching the clock?

Appreciate. Reciprocate. And get him to empty the damn Diaper Genie.

One idea for both of you: Try saying "thank you" to each other occasionally but not only in the big, typical thank-you moments. A random act of gratitude goes a long way when your patience has run thin, and since babies eat patience and breast milk for breakfast, lunch and dinner, I recommend you stock up on gratitude.

He should not make you "just deal with it."

Our kids were running around the beach house one summer morning.

It was day one of a long weekend vacation, right around breakfast time, and our toddlers were doing their toddler thing: refusing to listen to our pleas that they use their indoor voices and asking for hash browns over and over as if we might have been deaf the first 37 times they asked. We were setting up for a day full of laughter and playing and tears.

While the children were distracted by the smell of hash browns and fruit, I turned to my wife, sensing a brief break in the action.

"Can I take a quick shower?" I asked.

"Sure," she said with a nod, as she reached down to pick our daughter up for the umpteenth time that morning, as it's widely known that all children cease to have the ability to use their own legs at the exact moment their mother enters the room.

This was an innocuous and quick exchange, and it might sound a bit silly to mention it.

1. Why did I pick that moment to ask to take a shower?
2. Why did I ask? I'm a grown-up, after all.
3. Why did my wife not bat an eye at me leaving her alone with the kids?

The answer to all of this is rooted in an approach that has worked well for us as our babies grew from infants into toddlers.

Mutual respect for each other's needs.

My wife knows that I wouldn't be asking if I didn't already appreciate what I was asking her to do. I needed her to watch all the kids early in the morning while I got to enjoy some silence and a nice warm shower. It's not a fair exchange, and we both know it.

My wife also knows that I will return the favor, no questions asked, whenever she's ready. It might be 20 minutes later. It might be that night, meaning I might clean up the kitchen after dinner while she takes a long hot shower. But it's all "pay it forward" when it comes to a great parenting arrangement.

My wife knows that part of the reason I asked is that I want to show her that I'm respecting our unspoken process. I don't want to just disappear without a word, forcing her to just "deal" with the situation.

I also asked because I wanted to give her a chance to say no, in case she already had a plan in place and needed me to adjust. The simple act of asking, even if it's more formality than permission (we're adults, after all!), is all about *acknowledgment*. We're acknowledging each other's role. We're recognizing that life is a little nicer and kinder when you don't just blaze through your own way, disregarding how it impacts others. We're consciously and sometimes subconsciously trying to say, "I appreciate you, so I want to check in."

A parenting scenario where one of you constantly has to "just deal with it" is going to lead to burnout and resentment and exhaustion. You can't be balanced! For instance, if he's regularly running out to watch the game without seeing if you need anything (even if it's just a few hours to yourself), that's shitty. If he's not giving you a heads up when he needs to come home late from work and therefore you're stuck with a crying baby even longer than you thought you'd be, that's disrespectful. Do not tolerate it.

Moms already handle so much. One study showed that being a mom is the equivalent of working 98 hours per week! *(This is according to a 2017 study commissioned by Welch's of moms of 5 - to 12-year-olds.)*

Also, the "Just tell me what to do and I'll do it" line isn't helpful either, because now you have to make him a list. This is just another task that falls to you. That's not a partnership. That's more like hired help.

He can't ignore your feelings. He can't pretend that his actions don't impact you. **EVERY action he takes impacts you, even more so when you have a kid.**

I'm not saying he should ask permission like a 16-year-old asking if he can take the family car out for his date.

I'm saying that there needs to be an acknowledgment that he isn't living in a vacuum. It's not a hard thing to say "Hey, I was planning on an extra hour at work. I know you've had a long day. What can I grab on the way home?"

You may say no — "For God's sake, don't stop. Just get home, babe!" — but at least he'd be recognizing that you count on him being home at a certain time.

If you find that this is an area that's sorely lacking, it can help to have a nonchalant conversation about it. This is where you tell him that you're both trying to adjust to this new schedule and that it helps when you have a better idea of what he's trying to accomplish. A higher level of communication will be mutually beneficial. Trust me.

I'd suggest not bringing it up in the heat of the moment, though, because that will likely lead to defensive reactions. He won't be ready to listen to what you need.

Whether it's fitting in a shower during a busy morning or needing a night with the guys, the more that your husband can be in a mindset of mutual respect instead of one that expects you to "just deal with it," the better off you'll be. Guys are notoriously bad at barreling through life with blinders on and not thinking of how what we do impacts others.

He doesn't get to do that anymore.

5

From pregnancy to delivery day.

Your partner is your best advocate.

Delivery day is the time when your partner can really shine.

Wait, hold on. Don't yell at me. Let me preface that.

You are going to be the one to shine, mama.

You're gonna knock this shit out of the park. You've got this, and you're going to surprise yourself of what you're capable of doing.

(And, if you've already delivered and are just reading this out of curiosity, congratulations! You did it! You're one badass mama, and your baby thanks you!)

Meanwhile, dads are now so well known for being useless on delivery day that you don't even have to set up the joke in a comedy. You just put a dad in the delivery room and everyone knows what happens next. There's an entire episode of *Friends* about this, I think.

While some guys will be there every step of the way, from Lamaze class to fetching your ice chips, others don't take the hint. You want someone to hold up your leg while you push, and he's in the corner rooting for a touchdown.

I wish I could say that's a gross exaggeration of a stereotype, but I know a dad or two who have done that exact thing.

Let's acknowledge that some dudes are gonna pull a Michael in *The Office* during the fire drill scene and run out screaming, "Every man for himself!" They might be great at other things, but they suck at this. Asking for a wholesale change in attitude is likely going to end in failure. Selfishness doesn't change that easily.

This chapter, instead, is for the many guys who *can* shine during these earliest moments of fatherhood. They just need guidance, because you know what? You might be surprised at what he can accomplish, too.

He wants to keep you smiling (or, at least, reduce your grimacing). He wants to help alleviate your stress. He wants to put all of those childbirth techniques into practice so he can show you how committed he is. You went to all of those classes together. Now it's time for them to pay off.

In a sense, neither of you really know what you're doing, and you're both a combination of scared and nervous. You're doubly nervous because of the physical side of childbirth and, let's be real, who wouldn't be? It would be great if he could be your reassuring, steady rock. He's had a bit of practice at that, I hope. Prior to this moment, throughout your pregnancy, there were plenty of opportunities for him to improve his skills in the art of comforting you as you dealt with morning sickness, body aches, not being able to tie your own shoes, etc.

My wife came fully prepared for OB-GYN appointments for both pregnancies. She had a list of questions always at the ready, and I wouldn't have expected less from her.

Even then, we'd get unexpected bumps in the road (OB-GYN appointments should really be called "This Is Normal, Please Don't Panic" appointments). Our son, Elliott, was a little behind on development when he was in the womb, and one twin had an elevated heart rate a time or two. When they are so tiny and fragile, every single thing that's not a textbook case makes you want to bust out WebMD and scream at the doctor, "IS IT CANCER? DOES HE HAVE THREE HEADS? GIVE IT TO ME STRAIGHT, DOC!" while the doctor stutters "I was just checking your temperature!"

Dad skills start developing during each trimester, at each appointment and with each squeeze of the hand during those longest seconds of your life when the ultrasound tech is looking for your baby's heartbeat. Already, your dude is figuring out that you don't give a shit about anything else that day if something is a little off during a check-up. If he's smart, he'll be right there with you, doing his research or listening while you go over what the doctor said, rather than brushing it off as "not a big deal." It *is* a big deal. It's your baby. Everything is a big deal.

This is one of the many reasons I think that, if work permits, dads need to be at every single appointment. It's not just the mom's job, and, again, it's not like *you* can skip out and he can go solo.

"Sorry, my wife couldn't make it. She had to work. But let's see what this baby is doing!" *Lifts shirt up.*

Going to the OB-GYN together sets the standard that medical stuff with your baby is *both* of your responsibilities. Hopefully, the doctor you're meeting with is also the one who will help deliver your baby (although we were zero for two on that one). In the case that your doctor *will* be present at your delivery, it will be super important for your partner to know him or her and how they approach childbirth. Is this the kind of doctor who is overtly pushing for medications and interventions? Does he do a bad job of explaining what's going on? Is she the cheerleading type, or is she all business all the time? He should know.

But that's just the OB-GYN.

Going to a childbirth class together? Even better.

Childbirth: Prepare as a team.

I took several classes with my wife to get ready to be a dad:

- Birth preparation
- CPR/child safety
- Breastfeeding support

You know why I didn't give it a second thought? Because I had no idea what I was doing, and this was an opportunity for a crash course. I had barely even held a baby before my son was born, so I welcomed any advice. Even just seeing other dads there was reassuring, and some of those dads are still my friends to this day!

If you're looking for a way to kick-start involved parenting with your partner, childbirth classes are it. At the very least, they can provide reassurance for him. Once you're expecting, a parent feels like they are supposed to know all this stuff, which, as you know, is overwhelming. I can remember going to ultrasound appointments and kind of nodding like I knew what goes where and talking about how I wanted to be there during the delivery like I had any idea what it would be like. It's not like I had heard any stories from new dads about what it's actually like. I had heard zero stories, in fact. Zero stories from dads about what it was like in the delivery room or the days right after. It's not like guys couldn't talk about it. It just never came up.

Do you know what a perineum tear is, for example? Because I sure as hell didn't. (Do not Google that at work.)

The holistic childbirth preparation class we took was a huge confidence booster for me as a new dad, and my wife gave it kudos too. While there are many styles of childbirth classes, it was worth it for us to pay a little more to take a class that emphasized having the parents lead the discussion with the medical team on what we wanted when it came to delivery. That also helped me feel like I had a role. I learned so much it was ridiculous, from ways to soothe the baby to what to expect at childbirth, including what the baby will look like. (As a heads up, the "newborn baby" you see on TV is likely a three-month-old, because a bluish, sticky baby isn't cute.)

Childbirth class is not a big, slapstick group exercise of pushing out the baby like I thought it might be. When you hear "a dad at childbirth class," what's in your head is probably some sitcom trope of a flustered dad bobbling a plastic baby and trying to do Lamaze breathing. Yes, I did see a video of a woman giving birth. No, none of the guys passed out while viewing it, and watching the video was kinda comforting, to be honest. I could clear that hurdle before it was time for The Main Event, but let's be clear. Nothing can truly prepare you for watching a baby come out of your wife's vagina. At least I wasn't entirely in the dark, though!

Most of the class involved having conversations about our worries, learning techniques to help with labor and getting familiar with the jargon. Also, you'll say the word "placenta" a lot.

By the time we were in a delivery room the second time, when our twin girls were born, I felt like a pro. I credit childbirth class for a lot of that. And that's considering my daughter, Hannah, came out feet first. To be fair, nothing prepares you for seeing your daughter's leg dangling out of your wife's pelvis. My wife had already pushed out the first baby, and, as it happens with twins, that gave the second baby a ton of newfound room to go "Weeee!!!!" as she floated around waiting for her turn to travel through the birth canal. Hannah's foot came out first, and the nurse and I exchanged a look I'll never forget as we both said, "Uh ... push!"

The doctor, knowing my wife really didn't want a C-section, was a champ under pressure. She reached all up in my wife's business and essentially yanked Hannah out by the legs.

It was nuts and yet everything worked out. I credit going to childbirth classes and being involved at the OB-GYN for helping me feel less overwhelmed. This made me a better partner in moments of tension. The last thing my wife needed was for me to freak out!

Childbirth class doesn't need to be scary for either of you. It doesn't need to be uncomfortable. It's just new. And that's totally fine. It's supposed to be new! If you knew what was happening in childbirth, you wouldn't be going, unless you're one of those people who does things just to brag about it, and in that case, nobody likes you.

The class instructors are trained to make you feel welcome and involved, and men get reminders that their role is to be the rock; the guy who is there for you every step of the way.

Unless he's destined for a different category.

I saw up close how guys were approaching childbirth.

Looking around the childbirth class, it seemed to me that guys fall into one of two buckets:

The Involved Dad: He was asking questions. He was grabbing a pillow for his wife's back. He was not checking his watch or phone every five minutes. He would light up when someone asked him about becoming a dad. These guys were destined to be up for 3 a.m. feedings and wearing their own diaper bag.

The "My Wife Made Me Come Here" Dad: He looked like learning about this stuff was either useless or stupid or both. When he was asked about the baby, he'd only reply that he hoped the baby would be good at sports. He is checking ESPN on his phone right this second.

I saw one of those "My Wife Made Me" Dads smoking outside the baby class next to his pregnant wife.

If you're smoking beside your pregnant wife while attending CPR/child safety class, you may want to just call it a day because wow. You suck.

Also, it's not enough for him to just show up. Don't you dare accept that from your partner. You're not asking him to donate a kidney. You're asking that, *just like you're being asked by society*, he learn a bit about keeping the baby he helped *make* alive and happy.

He needs to be involved, show some enthusiasm, ask questions and even be OK showing a little vulnerability on the ride home if he's feeling worried or anxious. That's the way to get the most out of it, and if you're going, why not get the most out of it?

Action step: On the way home, ask him what was the most surprising thing he learned. It should peel back his emotions a bit. He might give a small indication of what he's thinking and what he's concerned about. For example, if he says he's surprised that some parents have a birth plan and that their plan doesn't always get followed, that could indicate that he had thought that, if you both plan a little, you'd be all set, and now he's worried that might not be the case. If you know what his concerns are, you'll be able to better work together as you prepare for the Big Day.

The good news is that, if he goes at all without some kind of big fuss, he's already on the way to becoming the involved dad type. If that's your man, his willingness to attend childbirth class already signifies a strong step in the right direction. It shows he isn't likely to take a back seat when it comes to parenting.

Nice work if that's already happened. Go enjoy a fine non-alcoholic beer to celebrate, or, if your dude is like me, a nice Mike's Hard Lemonade because they are delicious and he has little shame.

Yeah, but do we really need a childbirth class?

Should you take a childbirth class? I bet he's asking, and out of the two of you, he's the one not loving the idea of attending (or paying) for one. It's not required, but it'll make your life *so much easier* later on. I would highly recommend it unless you've both been around babies your whole life. Let's be honest, though. If that were the case, you probably wouldn't be reading this book, now would you? Ha! Caught!

My wife and I had such a positive childbirth class experience because we found a class that reflected our values: We wanted to learn how to gain more control of the delivery room decision making, how to make sure our birth plan was being considered and how to enjoy the process as much as possible.

Let's be honest, though. It costs money to go to a childbirth class, especially one that fits you perfectly as a couple. I get that. (Although, you may be able to find a free one that's put on by a local nonprofit — Google it!) When you're buying stuff for the nursery or moving from an apartment to a house, or whatever else is financially impacting you before the baby arrives, and then you're thinking about paying for a class that in theory *could* help, it may seem easy to say, "I'm sure we can skip it."

I'm here to say: Don't skimp on the tires when you're buying a Mercedes.

Don't go into the last trimester assuming you can both just read a blog post or two, talk to your parents and then be ready. There's a baby coming, people. Like, a real human being. This is the exact time to spend a little money now to be better prepared later. Maybe you could even see if a relative will pay for childbirth class as a baby shower gift.

Side benefit: It's encouraging to go through the class and see all the other couples dealing with the same stuff as you. You'll hear them ask questions you've been wondering and have doubts that sound all too familiar, and after the class, you may even have some new friends who, surprise, are dealing with a newborn baby too! What could be better for you?

Delivery day is almost here. Now what?

When it comes to labor and delivery itself, I'll leave that to doctors and women who have far more experience and expertise than I do. As for the other stuff that surrounds and impacts that experience? That's where your dude can shine, and I'd love to help.

Your partner is going to want some ideas on how to get

prepared, and here's what I suggest.

Roles for Dad on delivery day

- **Birth Plan monitor.** The hospital staff really will read it, if nothing else so that they can ask you better questions about what kind of childbirth you're hoping for. If you do a hospital visit in advance, ask about their approach to birth plans, because if they say flat out that they won't look at them, that's a red flag. Be flexible, though. If there's an emergency situation, you're likely not going to have the scented candles and mood music childbirth that you're dreaming of. Your partner can make sure the plan is being followed as closely as possible and ask questions you may not think of because, well, you're a little busy. He is your advocate.

  Example: My wife really wanted to avoid a C-section with the twins. We put it in the birth plan, and I knew I needed to emphasize that at every possible opportunity, especially when our daughter decided to flip around backward and a C-section seemed more likely! While my wife *was* able to talk with the doctor in that moment (insane!), if she had been too overwhelmed, I would have known exactly what her wishes were. The plan was on my phone and we had a hard copy on hand.

- **Delivery room bouncer.** He can be in charge of notifying relatives and friends so that they can get there in time. Or, even more importantly, he's in charge of keeping those people away who DON'T get to be with you in the delivery room. He can be the bad cop, telling family or friends that they need to slow their roll and that the waiting room is the place for them, thanks. People can handle it. You get to call the shots, and he can be the mouthpiece. Also, by the way, anybody who puts up a fuss about getting access to you against your wishes has some serious priority problems.

- **Hospital bag grabber.** You could be in this for hours upon hours, but if you prepared properly, you'll have everything you both need. Pack it together as a mini bonding activity, cause shit gets real when you start doing that! It's smart for him to bring a few snacks for himself (and for you!) in case it's a long process. (Pro tip: It will probably be a long process.) He doesn't have to be a martyr and starve. It won't do anyone any good if things are going slowly and he gets irritable because he's hungry. Going to the cafeteria may be out of the question, so have him pack something he can eat in a pinch. This will avoid a hangry husband, which no one has time for, let's be real.

Go ahead and pack the diaper bag as well because #diaperbaglife is coming soon. Or you can be like me with our first-born. We were planning on packing the bag the very day my wife went into labor a few weeks early. So instead of the orderly, organized packing we had intended to do, I ended up running around our bedroom at midnight throwing random things in a bag. My wife kept saying, "We aren't even going anywhere yet! The contractions are far apart. We have lots of time!" To which I replied, "I'm not going to be that asshole husband who arrives with nothing in the bag for his wife!" She's really proud of me. I think.

- **Photographer.** Decide sometime in advance of when someone is positioned in front of your exposed crotch whether you want any photos in the delivery room and just how "realistic" you want them to be. If you *do* want photos, this role might be great for your husband, unless he's going to ruin it by trying to get you to smile through a contraction, which I believe justifies homicide. You know him best.

Here's the deal, though. If you want something beyond camera phone shots, that nice camera better be in the hospital bag — with new batteries and a memory card — or you'll never remember it. Do you want makeup on and a chance to clean up? Do you want a photo right after the baby is born, no matter what you look like? How soon do you want photos posted online? The more you talk this through, the less chance you have of being agitated. He doesn't want to agitate you. He wants to impress you.

· **Baby buddy.** My twin girls both needed the NICU. My wife and I agreed ahead of time that I'd never leave their sides so that they always had one of us around while she recovered. This is a good thing to discuss in advance because the need for NICU can arise very quickly and the hospital staff may rush off with the baby before you decide what to do. *Dads are very much entitled to stay with their newborn.* Don't let anyone tell you differently.

I will never forget watching a team of nurses and doctors work on my 3-pound 14-ounce daughters. They were both relatively healthy preemies, but even so, they seemed so fragile. Being there gave me a sense of purpose after feeling otherwise helpless while my wife pushed them both out like a rock star. Just as a reminder, nobody ever expects to end up with a baby in the NICU. It can be hard as hell, but if it happens, you'll find comfort knowing that those are some of the most incredible nurses and doctors, and that they are literally working around the clock to help your baby.

· **Hospital route navigator.** Maybe there's one road and it's your only option. Maybe you could take the turnpike or backroads, depending on the time of day. Maybe you need a backup hospital in case you're at work when you go into labor and work is 40 minutes away. Let him be in charge of Google mapping the hell out of this so that you have plans in place regardless of the scenario. While it's unlikely that you'll need some movie-esque dash to the hospital, if labor starts around rush hour, for example, it would be good to have an alternate route in mind so that, in the heat of the moment, he can just reflexively start driving. Which reminds me ...

· **Car seat installer!** This will feel strange at the time, but you need to bring the car seat *to the hospital.* Cause, uh, you'll have the baby coming home with you. Don't assume you can run home and get it or that you'll *want* to run home. Put your partner in charge of getting the car seat installed weeks ahead of the due date.

Not only will that give you time to have someone make sure it's properly installed (police and fire stations offer free checks), it will give you time to adjust to having that space occupied in your car. Don't forget that the baby will be rear facing! Perhaps your husband would also take charge of researching car seats for the baby registry. You really want to avoid buying a used car seat (safety features get upgraded all the time). One suggestion: Use a car seat that has seatbelt-like buckles to connect to the seat. You want this to be as easy for him to install as possible. Trust me, he'll be installing and reinstalling seats for years. Don't forget, even if it's freezing, no heavy coats for the baby underneath the seat straps! Use a blanket.

The delivery room is truly the first place a guy gets to show that he's ready for fatherhood, even if he's scared or anxious or freaked out. The stakes are as high as they've ever been, and he is going to want to be "good at this," whatever that might mean for him.

This does not mean that while you're trying to push a baby out of your vagina or that while you're having a baby pulled out of your stomach, you should be gingerly holding your partner's hand and making sure his feelings are OK.

"Enough about me. How are YOU feeling, babe?"

Good God, you're in the middle of being a superhero! Batman doesn't ask Robin how his anxiety is doing while he chases down The Riddler. (By the way, if a newborn is a Batman villain, it's definitely The Riddler. Toddlers are Two-Face. Teens are Mr. Freeze.)

If he's any kind of solid partner on delivery day, he'll be looking out for you while you're focused on what's best for the baby.

Help him help you.

Here are some ways that you can help nudge his good intentions toward actual, tangible helpfulness.

· **If he says, "What can I do to help?" tell him precisely what you need.** If you don't know exactly, that's OK, too. It's not your duty to know exactly what you need at all times. It's his job to be as prepared as possible to meet those needs when they arise. It just helps if you can keep him updated!

Be clear about what you need and want.

· **Put it on him to give status updates to family and friends via text or in the waiting room.** This is similar to the "bouncer" role, but as we know, phones can be just as much of an interruption or a distraction as someone's physical presence. Let everyone know in advance that your partner will be passing along updates whenever he has them. This way, you're not feeling pressure to respond to texts or answer your phone.

· **Let him support you.** This can be such a beautiful moment for you as a couple, and I hope that you'll be able to look back on your delivery as a time when your partner really came through for you. Resist the urge to be in charge of everything during these extremely unique hours, and choose to rely on him to take care of superfluous things. You're about to meet your baby! Relax and focus on your labor. Also, supporting you is a tangible way that he can feel connected to you and the baby during these first precious moments of parenthood. Invite him in by relying on him, emotionally and otherwise.

· **But don't be afraid to say "OK see ya."** If he's causing more harm than good while you're in labor or if he's too overbearing, too talkative, too critical, too "too," then it's "see ya later, pal!" The whole point is to deliver a happy, healthy baby, and maybe he's lost sight of that. If that means you need to tell him to back the hell up, he'll get over it. He can come back when he's ready to let it be about you and your baby.

I can't wait for you two to have this time together.

I've never been more impressed with my wife than when I

watched her give birth. Anything I did in that room paled in comparison to what she was achieving, but I'm so glad I was able to do my part to reduce her stress, even if it was only by a little.

Assuming you want him there beside you as you push, he's there to hold your hand, give you verbal support (which should not involve acting like an out-of-control football coach) and to do anything else you may need. In my case, a nurse and I held my wife's hands and also her feet so she could push against us. I hadn't known until that very moment that I'd have the opportunity to be so active in the process, but in hindsight, it makes a lot of sense! Honestly, I wouldn't have had it any other way.

Your guy is going to be asked a million times, "Are you going to watch the baby come out?" and his knee-jerk response might be "Hellllllllll no!"

I'd like to suggest he does watch. Why? One, he'll likely only see something as miraculous and insane as a baby entering this world once or twice in his whole life. Also, unless you're doing the mirror thing, you won't be able to see it yourself, and I bet at some point you'll want to know what it was like.

(If he *does* decide to watch, he should be prepared that the baby's head might have a bluish tint, and that's OK.)

Two, if he watches, he'll be able to encourage you when you're almost there, in those final moments before you've completed one of the most physically taxing experiences of your life. He'll be able to cheer you on in real time and let you know how things are looking. Or he'll know when to keep his big mouth shut, like in the case of Hannah's birth, when I saw that foot pop out first, but I kept it to myself because that shit was crazy.

What else should your partner know when it's delivery day?

- **This is not about him.** It's about you and your baby. He should in no way attempt to steal the attention.
- **I don't care if his favorite team is on the one-yard line about to win the Super Bowl, if your baby is coming out, he better not be checking the TV or looking at his ESPN app.** I mean, he can do that if he's hoping for a divorce, I suppose. Yes, I have heard of dads who were checking scores during delivery, but he sure as hell better not be *acting* like he's involved when he's actually half-watching a game. "Daddy missed your birth because the Steelers dropped an interception and he was sulking." If you nodded your head because this bullet point sounds way too likely, make it clear ahead of time that you need his 100% focus for this.
- **It's OK if he's feeling nervous or even scared!** As I've said, nothing can totally prepare either of you for what you're about to experience, and that's part of what will make the day so incredible. It will be entirely unique to the two of you and the family that you're creating. Your best bet for taking control of those nerves is preparation and communication. You've got this! Both of you need to know that the day your baby arrives will be one of the most memorable and unbelievable days of your life, but it's only the beginning.

Any guy can pull his shit together for one day and be Mr. Dad.

What you need is Mr. Everyday Dad.

And that starts right away. Those on-call nurses and 24-hour support at the hospital? It's amazing how fast that goes away and how fast it's just the three of you, *in it,* ready or not.

* * *

Bonus content: Six things you think you're going to need as a new parent that are a big no from me, dawg.

1. **Baby wipe warmers:** These are a scam. There's no way of proving they really make a difference beyond the placebo effect, and as long as you aren't storing your wipes in the freezer, they will likely be room temperature. However, *do* remember to bring the diaper bag in from the car when there are extreme temperatures! Otherwise, you'll be trying to do a diaper change in the backseat with frozen wipes. Or so I've heard. You also don't want extreme heat messing with butt paste, etc. There's nothing that will ruin your husband's mood more than melted, oozing butt paste all over his new leather interior.

2. **4,128 newborn outfits:** Part of the fun of having a baby is dressing them up, taking a million photos of them crying so you can post the one photo where they look more confused than pissed and then showing off your beautifully attired child to the world. I'm not saying not to do that. Do it! It's fun! But you need, like, five outfits for that stuff, not including major holidays. You can buy your two-month-old daughter all the dresses you want, but they are impractical when you're changing a diaper 10 times a day. It's white onesies. Over and over. You're not letting anyone down. You're being practical. It will also be helpful to your husband when he's trying to change a blowout for your three-week-old baby girl *not* to be wearing a four layer gown.

3. **Buckets of toys for your baby:** Phase them in! People will want to buy your kid toys, because that's more fun, but they will only ever use two or three at a time, max.

Ask for diapers! Always ask for diapers! Don't let your house become overrun with toys that don't get played with. You're causing unnecessary stress, and for what?

4. **Baby proofing ... when the baby doesn't even crawl yet.** A dad's job most likely is going to involve baby proofing. I can attest that the drawer stoppers were invented in Satan's workshop, and I hate installing them almost as much as I hate installing car seats. Please remember that you're soooooo far off from needing to baby proof every corner of your home! If they can't crawl, they don't need drawer stoppers and baby gates. If they can't walk, they don't need the fireplace covered in styrofoam. Don't add more tasks to an already full to-do list before it's necessary.

5. **Fancy (insert thing here).** Some things are worth paying retail price to buy new. Car seats (A must! And do yourselves a favor and get one that clicks in easily to the seat anchors with push button release). A crib, as some older ones may not have been built to meet newer standards. Maybe a stroller. But for most things, you can get by with hand-me-downs, borrowing from a friend whose kid is now a toddler, or just riding it out to see if you need it at all. All of the merchants of the world are going to throw tons of marketing at you in an effort to convince you that you need every item ever invented or your baby will suffocate and never go to college. Relax. Save your money. Ask yourself if this will truly make a difference. Will it be useful beyond a couple of weeks or make your life that much easier? Great. If not, get by with what works.

6. **Four different strollers.** Or any variation of the same baby item. We purchased multiple strollers for our twins only to

discover that we really only ever used the jogging stroller because it was the simplest! Try some out! Borrow a few! Get one off Craigslist if you need to try one without making a big investment, and then, if you love it, you can always buy the brand-new version that will last a long time for multiple babies. Baby steps, so to speak. The same goes for having a bouncer *and* a swing *and* a mamaRoo *and* a Pack 'n Play. It's doubtful you'll use all of them enough to justify the cost as well as the space they take up. What's more, your baby may scream like a banshee in one or the other of them, rendering it useless, no matter how much it cost you. Babies have preferences, you know, and babies do not give a shit what you spent. Babies don't give a shit about a lot of things.

6

... and the crazy days after.

The birth of your kid is just step one. What comes next is what makes (and in some cases) breaks a dad.

"Am I going too fast?" I asked my wife.

Our son was strapped into the brand-new car seat that I had painstakingly installed in our SUV not long before.

Did you know that you aren't allowed to leave the hospital until you can show that you have the car seat installed properly?

It might be the only official test you have to pass to demonstrate that you have any clue how to be a parent before you're allowed to leave with your baby. "We're not letting you take this cute baby home until you can at least prove that you can pull a strap and use a latch."

I distinctly remember that I was wearing a faded red hoodie. Usually, I err on the side of being somewhat put together, and hoodies are more of a "mowing the lawn" kind of deal. But, after a couple of long nights at the hospital where we painstakingly worked to try and figure out how to nurse (her) and swaddle (me), we were exhausted and ready to go home.

By "ready," I mean that the insurance company told the hospital that we had to go home. We would have gladly offered to pay rent and stay there if it meant we could have kept those helpful nurses around forever.

Alas, at some point after delivery, you have to leave.

You have to be a parent. Inside the hospital, where a staff of health professionals is paid to give you trusted advice and medical assistance, you're not so much a parent as you are a kid at an intensive summer camp learning a new skill.

But then you leave camp. And you're expected to do the thing, whether you're ready or not.

My mom likes to say that she "launched" me when I started college. It's her way of saying that I was officially an adult and that she had spent years preparing me so now it was my turn to figure things out.

The hospital launched the hell out of us.

So, there I was, slowly inching the car through the parking lot with my wife beside me and the most important passenger of my entire life strapped in behind me. In hindsight, it's surprising that I didn't have bubble wrap and duct tape on hand.

I remember getting honked at as we drove home, and it was like I had achieved a badge of honor.

Maybe that's the moment your partner will feel like a father.

Maybe it will be when he holds your son or daughter for the first time.

It's all such a blur to me. I wish I could remember it more clearly. Our son came out into the world and a small team of medical professionals checked his vitals and warmed him up a bit as I observed (I say "observed" as if I would have offered any observation beyond "HOLY SHIT THIS IS NUTS!"). My wife was still in the hospital bed, delivering the placenta. Somehow, they never show that part in movies. You work so hard to deliver a baby, and, surprise, you aren't even done yet! Now you gotta push out an organ.

One thing that I do vividly remember is the moment when the doctor put Elliott on my wife's chest for the first time. How she teared up. How she looked like she had never been so in love in her entire life. How she was 100% *mom* right then, right there, and how I knew that she would have done anything for that squirmy, squishy little baby.

For me, it took a bit longer for all of it to soak in. I was a dad, for sure. But I didn't transform into a "real" dad until after those first few weeks of changing diapers and feeding and nonchalantly talking about breast milk like I used to talk about the Steelers. It was tangible.

Because the delivery day is one thing. The days *after*? Those are the days that truly reveal what parenthood is all about.

Your guy will see that parenting is not those first few moments in the hospital with balloons and flowers and nurse check-ins. That's just the congratulatory stuff. It's such a proud moment, but just like Christmas morning, it's over in the blink of an eye.

That first day with your baby is magical and difficult and heartwarming and confusing. It's a lot! And in the following weeks, it can feel like you're living in an alien world. Guys, in particular, will wonder how they're supposed to do all of this stuff that they've never done before.

That's in part because all of the support seems to slowly dissipate as you go along, save for a few family members or best friends.

It's kinda like announcing your first pregnancy compared to

subsequent pregnancies.

The first announcement will inevitably get all the deserved pomp and circumstance, including baby showers where you're likely to receive that wipe warmer that I warned you about. (Believe me, people only buy wipe warmers for someone's first baby.) You get to feel like the queen, and all eyes are on you. Your Facebook post blows up. You're the center of attention, and you even get your own parking spot at the grocery store for expectant moms!

Then baby number two or three or four comes around. You still get the special parking spot, but the excitement from friends and family might be noticeably decreased. You've done this before, and the offers to help or make a big fuss subside. I don't know if you know this, but the baby shower gets downgraded to a "baby sprinkle" the second time around. I guess the third one is a baby trickle? By the second and especially the third, the pregnancy announcement settles into the same social impact territory as "I got a new job!," "We bought a house!" and eventually "We just won $3 on a scratch off!"

By this point, people are excited for you, sure, but your community of friends and family won't quite come together in the same way to throw their full support behind you and make sure you're absolutely prepared. It's kinda nuts, speaking as someone with three kids, because having three is 413,179% harder than having one. We should all make a BIGGER deal out of the third or fourth or fifth pregnancy! But we don't.

Similarly, delivery day is a monumental occasion. But, man, we'd all be better off if all of the support and visits and focus came in the subsequent days. On delivery day, you have a team of nurses and doctors on hand. You don't even have to change the baby's diaper if you don't want to. It's during the ensuing days when you realize how much you value and need the help.

It is an absolute miracle any time *anyone* can get pregnant. Sure, we toss around the word "miracle" a lot — especially in relation to sports feats — but the idea that your body is able to use another person's body fluid combined with your egg to create something that 16 years from now won't look up from their phone to say goodbye to you ... I mean, that is an absolute blessing! It's the miracle of life, but once those fleeting days of "congratulations" texts, baby showers and the endless string of strangers touching your belly are over, and delivery day has come and gone, and somehow maternity leave (and paternity leave, if you're lucky) is winding down, then what?

Here's when having help will really make the difference between staying somewhat sane and driving away in the middle of the night to join the circus because anything would be better than this, thankyouverymuch.

You'll have so many people offer to help early on, likely because you were there for them when they had a major event (hello, never-ending bachelorette parties!), and in a perfect world, before the baby even arrives, you'll have a few conversations with friends to see what they're up for, especially if they've taken care of a baby in the past or are a mom themselves.

Can't figure out which way the diaper goes? No problem! You're new at this! Here, let me help.

Have no idea how to get the baby to take a consistent nap? No worries, here are 218 relatives available to hold the baby non-stop so that he never touches the ground long enough to even get tired.

Feeding has turned you into a bottle washing machine who

doesn't have time to make dinner? A casserole is headed your way, Champ! No worries!

Let me just say, though, that not all "help" is good help. For example, this is not the time to see if your notoriously unreliable but totally fun friend wants to step up. They will likely *not* step up and you will be sleep-deprived, and that's a recipe for a wave of passive-aggressive texts, which, let's be honest, you will not have time for.

What to do when your friends offer to help:

- **Get a date written down.** It's nice for someone to say, "Just let me know when I can help!" The problem with that, however, is that it isn't actually helpful. Now they've given you a chore. Now, at some point, when you're leaking from every orifice and the baby is crying too and you're elbow deep in a sink full of dirty dishes, you have to have the wherewithal to grab your phone and send a text. Instead, right at the moment they offer, give them a date and a timeframe. "Yes! This Thursday afternoon, can you come over and watch the baby for two hours?" Have a few days and times in mind that generally work for you so that, when someone asks, you don't have to get back to them.
- **This is not a fun visit!** Have them do laundry/wash dishes/give the baby a bottle. They aren't there to "ooh" and "aah." That's not helpful. That's you entertaining them. You are not in a state to entertain. Sure, they'll see the baby! But there will be other times to cuddle and hold him. Right now, you and your partner need help. Don't feel awkward about asking for genuine help, either. This is not the time to feel insecure about your relationships. Good friends will follow through. Great friends will do even more than that.

- **Not sure what to ask?** Think about creating time, rather than a checklist. Time seems to disappear when you're caring for a newborn. Having an extra set of hands can help reduce that! Have your friend take the baby for a stroller ride while you nap for an hour and then drop the baby off with a simple goodbye because that's what you need. See if your girlfriend will come to Target with you and stay in the car with the baby while you run in and grab a few things. It's amazing how difficult it can feel to complete a quick grocery run when you know that getting the baby out of the car will wake her up. My wife has sat in a parking lot more times than she can count, just waiting for one of our babies to wake up!

- **Be wary of anyone who doesn't seem up to provide real help. It's not rude to decline a visit.** You can politely put them off until the baby is a little older and you've got a routine in place. Unless it's a close relative, you have no real obligation. Feeling at the end of your rope but also obligated? See if your partner can be the designated guest greeter while you conveniently run out for an errand. He can show off the baby and you can grab a cat nap in a parking lot or sip a cappuccino.

We've had so many friends help over the years, and I'm telling you that the relationships forged in the fires of early parenthood last forever. I will never, ever forget a coworker who once came to my aid. Our girls were just babies and my son was about three years old. During that season, we usually didn't even try asking anyone to watch them all by themselves because it was such an undertaking!

On this day, however, I was out of options. I was getting

ready to be interviewed for a promotion at work, and my wife was supposed to meet the babysitter at our house to switch off. Unfortunately, though, she got stuck behind an accident at the beginning of a bridge that rerouted traffic on a busy highway through a tiny town, causing her to be delayed for hours.

My coworker, who happens to also be an amazing grandmother and human being, answered my frantic text asking if she could drop everything and drive to my house, where she had never been, and babysit my kids, whom she had only seen a few times. She did. I got the job and a tangible reminder of how important it is to surround yourself with good people.

Most of the time, though, you won't have last second requests for help come through, and, of course, it's only natural that the help will eventually trickle off. While people will rally around you in the early going, most people are going to move on with their lives. They'll check in, of course! They're still great friends or wonderful siblings, but unless they're living with you, it would be impossible for them to offer truly beneficial help every day.

In many ways, parenting can be one of the loneliest things you'll ever do, even as you're constantly surrounded by others.

When the grandparents go back home, the friends go to work and the initial rush of adrenaline fades, you might feel shocked at just how *different* things are now, how much nonstop effort is needed and how you need, more than ever, to feel like you're on the same page as your baby's father. A truly amazing partner can be a lifesaver.

When you have a great partnership, you can get through the chaos ... and even grow to appreciate it.

Still, you have to be honest with yourselves about what you're facing.

Parenting little kids can be a tornado full of knives and grenades and poop.

"Why didn't anyone tell us that at some point as a parent, you would be pooping and throwing up at the same time and that you'd still have to get up with your @%*&$@% kids at 5 a.m. the next morning to make breakfast?"

This very graphic question posed by my flu-ridden wife begs for follow up, namely, "Um, are you OK? Do you need me to call a doctor?"

But it's also a fantastic question because I can tell you with certainty that no one ever prepared us for that side of parenthood. We had read lots of books. We had jokingly watched *What to Expect When You're Expecting*. We had talked to friends. We were mostly prepared for the diapers, the late nights, the calling other parents by their kid's name because that's as far as you got — "Hi, Jill's dad!"

If you're not this far into parenting yet, you need to know that this side of having kids exists. And it's headed your way.

You and your partner need to be aware in case you were blissfully thinking you'd be the kind of parents who will somehow avoid all that stuff *other* families get by simply keeping your kids healthy with vitamins, hand sanitizer and essential oils.

Myths that those types of parents believe:

1. **We'll never get sick at the same time as our baby because we "don't get sick."**
   Hahahaha! Oh damn, you're dumb. You are definitely going to get sick as a new parent. You're going to get sick all the time. You'll be wiping other people's snot with your bare hands with such regularity that you'll have to remind

yourself to use a Kleenex on yourself.

If you have your kid at daycare or the church nursery or in any other type of group care situation, you need to know that that's where the Ebola virus, staph infections and influenza have their best parties. If you're anything like me, you'll start seeing all the -ologists and -iatrists so often that, if you get one more hole punched, your next appointment will be free. I drink hand sanitizer on the off chance that it will disinfect my insides where, to be frank, there's probably baby poop somewhere.

2. **We pick up the slack for the other person, so it's not a big deal.**

That's super cute that you think your spouse won't get sick. Of COURSE he will. He isn't walking around in a hazmat suit.

Also, I'm assuming that you touch him at some point during the day and that he doesn't keep your kids at arm's length like that captain from *The Sound of Music*. Can we just take a second and acknowledge that Captain von Trapp was a real dick as a dad? Great hair but a real dick. #uninvolveddadalert

3. **We'll never get pooped on and thrown up on in the same day or maybe even the same hour.**

Let me paint a picture. When our son was our only child, he came down with a nasty flu. As in, "coming out both ends" nasty. (P.S. if all of this poop and throw up talk makes you queasy, I've got bad news for you. You're about to start using diarrhea in conversations like some people use "literally.")

So my son had been sick but seemed to be recovering. I had gotten him all ready for bed, and as I was rocking him, it

became apparent that, like Missy Elliott does with music,*
I was about to lose control over my entire body. (* High
five yourself if you got that reference.)

I literally had to toss him in the crib — and I mean there
could have been orange cones waving him in with the
landing that was involved — and race over to the bathroom
where I barely made it to the sink before losing it like a
prequel to *Bridesmaids*. The worst part, though, was that
my wife had ALREADY come down with the flu and had
quarantined herself in our master bath, which I believe
she later called a war zone. Thankfully, I had a few loving
family members around that day who were able to clean
up the messes because we couldn't move.

And guess what? The next day, Elliott didn't wake up
saying "Hey guys! Heard you had a rough night so I slept
until nine. I'll grab my own waffles." Nope. He still woke
up throughout the night. He still expected waffles in the
morning. Somehow, you just figure out a way to make it
work. (One thing that helps is if you take as realistic an
approach as possible. Prepare as much as you can before
you start getting sick yourself. I recommend prepping
food, getting outfits ready, whatever you know you won't
want to do the next day.)

Unfortunately, that scenario has happened more than once
for us. When one of our kids gets sick now, we start a
mental countdown of how long we'll continue wearing
pants before it becomes not worth the effort. One by one,
we fall. I could bathe in Z-Packs and it wouldn't matter. I
spent half of January catching throw up in my hands.

4. **Eh, how bad can one day of sickness be?**

A day is a matter of perspective. Today? Pretty quick. But

when you're crawling — actually crawling — to get to the nursery to help your baby because your legs are worthless from Jackson Pollacking your toilet, a day can be pretty long.

You may make it through the first year of having a baby without the two of you coming down with something that bad. But the day will come. It's a badge of honor, and the badge is made of tears, ginger ale and crackers.

5. **Other parents are just being dramatic. I've been sick before, and it's not a big deal.**

   Right, just the same way other parents are being dramatic about how tired they get because how bad can it be? It's not like you fall asleep standing up or dream of going to bed all day. Just sleep when the baby sleeps! If the baby naps while you drive, you nap while you drive!

OK, now you know that it can get intense and that it can feel like you're on a reality show. But here's the thing. It's doable! It's totally doable. And worth it, I promise.

Embrace the crazy. You're doing great.

"Now I can see what it's really like," my aunt said during a visit a few years ago.

My son was jumping from one piece of furniture to another. My then-one-year-old daughter was trying to put a hole in the fireplace. Her twin sister was crying about, well, let's go with the idea that perhaps the air brushed against her face or some other totally legitimate crisis of the moment.

It was a weekday evening. My wife was at work, and my mother-and-law and my aunt were hanging out at our house.

My aunt lives across the state so she mostly sees the kids through Facebook photos.

"I see them online, of course, but you don't really get a sense of what you're dealing with until you see them in person," my aunt said, as a baby crawled over her like itsy bitsy spider crawling up the water spout.

Then and now, it's controlled chaos, and by that point in our parenting journey, my wife and I barely blinked at it.

Here's what I need you to know: No one has it all handled.

Not parents with three kids. Not those friends with a baby who only appears to take naps and giggle, if Instagram is to be believed. Not expectant parents who have the nursery in Pinterest shape with five months to go. Not celebrity parents.

No one has kids who always wake up happy, eat all their meals, practice their Mandarin, ask to take a bath, give you a kiss at night and sleep nine blissful hours only to start it all over again the next day.

No mom has the perfect husband or partner who would put Jack on *This is Us* to shame, either.

You know that, right?

You say you do. When you scroll through a flawless Instagram feed, you say, "These are just the highlights. I bet their kid is crazy."

But then you go back to your life and wonder why your baby only fusses in front of friends or why your toddler is the only one who isn't potty trained or why your kid lights houses on fire. True story: Our son accidentally almost burned down our house by stacking pillows next to the fireplace, and the pillows caught on fire!

At some point, you'll be trying to get your baby to eat solids, and you'll wonder if you'll be perceived as a failure if you confess that she refuses to eat, even though your negotiating skills rival those of Liam Neeson after his daughter was taken. The fact that I even felt I should use the word "confess," like you somehow did something "wrong," speaks volumes.

Please give yourself a pass.

Please give your partner a pass.

Please tell yourselves that it's OK and that you don't owe the world explanations or caveats or asterisks. You never have to say "He's normally not like this." All of our children are "like this" sometimes, and here's the thing: We're all in this together.

If you tell your kids that you love them and you try your best to make sure they're in a good position to succeed and more often than not you see them progressing toward becoming functioning adults, awesome. You did it! You won the parenting trophy.*

* There is no trophy, and that's something that needs to be corrected immediately. If my kids can get participation trophies for sports, I better get one for driving them there.

Here's what I can tell you about my kids when they were infants:

Hannah was a daredevil who thought stairs were a fun place to lean backward. She also walked around like a T-Rex rumbling toward your rearview mirror. In between adorable photos of her laughing her face off at something her brother did, she was likely mad that we took something away. Or she was throwing food. Or she was screaming at me while I rocked her to sleep because she was NOT tired.

And she's perfect.

Quinn is a middle child (by all of five minutes). She may be Hannah's twin, but that's about the only similarity. In between precious photos of her sucking her thumb as she nestled her head on my wife's shoulder or photos of her giggling at peek-a-boo, Quinn was likely refusing to eat anything we put out for dinner. Or she was whining because she hadn't been held in the past 30 seconds. Or she was wide awake for two hours in the middle of the night for no reason and would cry if you dared to put her back in her crib.

And she's perfect.

Elliott had the chubbiest legs you can imagine on a six-month-old baby. He was also colicky and spent what seemed like forever screaming and refusing to sleep. He needed to be fed breast milk through a tube and a syringe to help him gain weight, a process that meant his mother and I barely slept for weeks on end.

And he's perfect.

You can have perfect babies who still make you shout to no one in particular "What are you DOING!?!?" 10 times a day. There's no such thing as a family that runs smoothly. Some do it a little better than others, but you're fooling yourself if you believe someone who claims it's all snuggles and dry underwear all day every day.

After all, nobody gets a sense of what you're dealing with except you. All they see are the hugs and the smiles and the family vacation photos.

Year after year, it's the controlled chaos that makes you a family. You and your husband are in this together, and you will get through the rough times. They don't last forever, I promise. Babies do eventually go to sleep. They do eventually eat properly. They do eventually stop needing 10 diaper changes a day.

That partnership you have, that mom-and-dad-are-a-united-front thing, that's what can help push through those early weeks and months when you're wondering how anyone survives this.

I'm far from a perfect father, and even when I feel like I'm on my "A" game, it doesn't always matter. Sometimes, my kids won't let me help and my wife has to do everything (and that can make her life very hectic). Recently, my son told me that he loves his mom "80 80 80 80 80 80 one million 80%," and loves me "1%." That tracks. He would go back inside her womb right now if he could. At some point, he'll probably flip and spend more time with me.

My daughters have made it seem like only mom can put on their socks, like mom went to Sock University or something.

But I still try, as do so many dads out there who recognize that fatherhood isn't like choosing produce at the grocery store. We don't get to only take the pretty parts or the parts that make us feel good about ourselves. On some days, they will cuddle up with me and whisper "I love you daddy" and everything is perfect, but that can't be the only motivation.

What you need and deserve is a guy who isn't waiting for a pat on the back or for his kids to validate him. He needs to dive right in and keep showing up, even (and especially) when it gets tough. No one would expect any less from you, right?

7

Who works? Who stays home?

What do you do about your jobs when maternity leave is over?

So, you're getting adjusted to a routine now that you're past those crazy early days because, as it turns out, you can't just set the baby under a heat lamp, install a hamster water dispenser and let the kid grow for 18 years until he's ready to go to college.

By now, you've undoubtedly figured this out. Pregnancy starts out with a yet-to-be-born baby who's constantly cared for and then poof, you're on the clock as soon as he comes out.

This is when it becomes time to make those major decisions that have the potential to alter your career, finances, mood, availability ... damn, basically everything!

Remember how I said that dads take longer to realize what exactly is going on? That continues well after you have the baby.

For dads, the timeline from pregnancy to "Oh shit, we have to take care of this baby?" is as follows:

- "We're having a baby!"
- "Holy #%#% we're having a baby."
- "I have no idea how to be a dad!" (This book might help.)
- "OK, let's do this. I'm ready to become a father."
- "Holy #%^&! What is coming out of my wife's body and what is that fluid?!?!"
- "This is the most beautiful little angel I've ever seen."
- "Wait, NOW what the #%^& is coming out of my wife's body? THAT'S a placenta? Oh my god, I need to buy my wife a push present."
- "I'm so happy to be a dad."
- "..."
- "..."
- "... Wait. How are we taking care of our baby?"

Your career and financial status are going to be impacted by growing your family. Guaranteed.

Think it's simple? Maybe, if you have clear-cut options, but who really has that?

In the coming chapters, we'll dive into how the baby impacts your marriage and personal life, but we can't just gloss over the financial side of things. Your guy is *definitely* thinking about this, whether or not he happens to be the primary earner in the household.

It doesn't have to overwhelm anyone. Somehow, someway, family after family find a way to make it work. Some families have privilege and luxury; they can use able-bodied family members for free daycare, they have flexible jobs that let them stay home as much as needed and they may not need a babysitter for years.

Some have to scrimp and save for every diaper. Childcare is a constant, real concern; a babysitter not showing up could mean that one parent misses a shift at work and risks losing their job. Financial stability becomes an even more glaring issue when you can't just avoid a cost, like you might with childcare.

Most of us, though, fall somewhere in the middle. We can't splurge on a full-time nanny. We may have a relative nearby but not one we'd use for daily care. We have to find something feasible that won't break the bank but also won't make us feel like we have to check *Dateline* every night to see if our childcare provider will be featured.

This is a perfect area for your guy to put his researching skills to good use. Use his keen interest in making sure you're all set financially to your advantage, and have him dive into childcare options.

Childcare: At some point, someone else will watch your baby.

Childcare is one of the biggest financial-related decisions you'll make about your baby.

You have to think about how childcare impacts you financially, logistically and even emotionally. Yes, the potential of hearing your baby scream because they don't want to be dropped off at a strange place* is something you will need to factor in. Not to mention the whole "What place is going to keep my baby safe and healthy?" thing.

* This doesn't last forever. My son clung to me like a barnacle on a ship for the first few weeks, but before long he would go "BYEEEEEEE!" It's comical now for me to think that at one point, I wasn't sure if he was ever going to be OK in daycare. If you're in that boat, it will get better. I promise. It's true that it's much harder on the parents. You stay calm, and they stay calm. At worst, they

calm down two minutes after you leave their sight.

Every family is unique, so creating a summary of the possible childcare scenarios is nearly impossible. In many cases, however, it comes down to the following two options:

Option 1: Both of you work. Your baby goes to full-time childcare.

PRO: You don't have to worry about a stalled career. This is especially a consideration for moms who are worried about being "mommy tracked." A female workforce study revealed about 11% of moms surveyed decided not to return to full-time employment after having a baby because they discovered they had been passed over for high-profile projects or offered less high-profile work. So if either of you feels like you have a boss who doesn't take kindly to people focusing on their families, well, first off, that's a huge red flag. In the short term, though, if that's your primary method of income, it could be a dealbreaker. This route keeps you both in the game.

PRO: Neither of you needs to feel like you "gave up" your career, which can help reduce resentment.

PRO: You'll maximize your earnings, although that's only if you find cost-effective daycare. You could be looking at tens of thousands of dollars for full-time care. If you both make about the same amount, it might be better for your bank account to hold onto your jobs. This is especially true if one of you has excellent insurance. That might be a reason for one person to keep their job even if they might be better at taking care of the baby. Insurance means a lot.

PRO: You get a reduction in the daily stress and strain of taking care of a baby around the clock. As a full-time worker outside of my home, I do get a mental baby break. Sure, I have stress from my job, but no one is screaming at me because they pooped themselves. Usually.

CON: Full-time daycare costs, and I'm rounding down here, are about eleventy billion dollars. It cost $9,000 to send our three toddlers to daycare just three mornings a week. The National Association of Child Care Resource & Referral Agencies reveals the average center-based daycare cost in the United States is $11,666 per year ($972 a month), but prices range from $3,582 to $18,773 a year ($300 to $1,564 monthly ... living in a city will get you). Think about that. As Care.com put it, nearly one in three families report spending 20% or more of their annual household income on daycare.

Do check for income-related discounts that some places, such as YMCAs, may offer. Also, some employers offer a Dependent Care FSA. It's a pain in the butt, yes. You've got to download forms, keep track of your balance, submit for reimbursement and so forth. What do you get for that? Pre-tax funding for daycare. It's like having a big 30% off coupon! Sure, 30% off coupons are usually more fun—Kohl's makes every coupon seem like a lottery ticket, and sometimes it's like Kohl's is paying *me* to shop—but it's real savings nonetheless.

CON: Unless your daycare is near where you work, you won't be able to see your baby all day, which can bring its own sense of guilt and emptiness.

CON: For some, it's tough to swallow that there's a really long stretch in the day where someone else will be taking care of all of your baby's needs. If you don't have much time off and your baby needs childcare at, say, four weeks old, before they can even lift their head (and reduce the chance of suffocation), you probably are feeling anxious about the mere idea. Remember, though, that these people are pros!

This is where getting references, making sure the childcare

providers have infant CPR training and all of the certifications needed, as well as having a good gut feeling pays off. You're allowed to be picky when it comes to daycare. This isn't ordering Chinese food. It's not like you can go cheap on childcare. They do *New York Times* cover stories about daycares like that. Do. Not. Skimp. On. Daycare.

Option 2: You work full-time. The other parent quits their job or drastically reduces their hours and takes care of the baby during the day.

PRO: You still have one full-time income with benefits—my God, insurance is important when you have a baby. Because of their need for emergency intervention and the NICU, my twins alone racked up over $200,000 in medical bills by the time they hit two months old. Without insurance, we'd have been screwed.

PRO: One of you gets to keep pushing forward on your career (and therefore improving your earning potential), and the other person gets the benefit of maximum bonding time with the baby.

PRO: You greatly reduce dependency on childcare; less cost, less guilt, less anxiety over someone else taking care of your baby, and you have a more flexible schedule.

CON: Depending on who's quitting their full-time job, there can be resentment. Unless you have established a mutual respect for each other's careers, any push for one person or the other to stay at home could be perceived as the other spouse not believing their career is "worth it."

Both of you need to think through who can leave their job with the least amount of negative consequences AND who would be able to best handle staying at home with the baby, which is no small task.

CON: You'll have less income, which on its own can cause ongoing stress. Depending on daycare costs where you live, you may find the lost income is still better than daycare expenses.

CON: One person staying at home puts the two of you in very different daily lives. One of you goes about your business and the other deals with all the highs and lows of taking care of a baby. A bad day for either of you can be tough to relate to by the other person. If and when you or your partner want to jump back into the workforce, there's now a gap in employment, which can make it tough to get hired again.

Here's how we do things in my house.

My wife and I went with option 2. For us, it was the best possible solution. We wanted to have one of us be with our son and eventually our daughters as much as possible. Our mindset was that we'd never get that time back with our babies. We did this knowing that we'd be greatly reducing our income, but for us, it's been worth it.

My wife left her full-time position at a college and now teaches English part-time. She also teaches fitness classes. She gets to be with our twins and our son every day, helping to mold them into thoughtful and loving people. We've still had to put our kids in daycare a few mornings a week, but we viewed that as a positive for everyone, even with the cost. Although I'm at work all day, I know that my wife or the daycare are looking out for what's best for my kids, and that's a great feeling.

It's still far from the perfect situation. Why? Because when you have a baby, you're going to feel like no matter what you decide there are drawbacks.

Our daily schedule is hectic, to say the least. We are fortunate to not have rigid schedules, but still it can be a constant headache. My wife teaches a few classes a week at a college plus teaches at a gym, and I have a day job, so we were still constantly picking up the kids or dropping them off with each other, especially in those first few years.

We have had to pay for daycare, and as I said, even though it's only part-time, it amounted to thousands of dollars per year. Some people opt to have a spouse stay home entirely, but as any stay-at-home parent knows, watching a baby is its own full-time job. Good luck getting anything done!

Also, I miss out on moments all the time. For example, when my son started saying some of his first words, I had to watch it via video. I missed his first bike ride too.

My wife had to take the majority of care of twin babies and a toddler during the day (and then we flip-flopped a lot at night). There's a reason every single person we bump into at the grocery store says, "You must have your hands full!" She also had to deal with work, so it had the potential to be stressful on both ends on any given day.

Would we change anything? No. We have beautiful, healthy, happy kids.

We have hustled and we have made the finances work, and we're fortunate that we even have the option to have one of us home at all for most of the day. In fact, you may be reading all of this and thinking to yourself, "Having one parent stay home isn't even an option for us." To that, I would say that whatever works best for your family is all that matters. Don't let others shame you. They are not in your situation.

Unfortunately in the United States, we're forced to make these decisions far too soon.

This is a problem in America more than in many other

countries where maternity and paternity leaves last six months, a year, or even longer. In the U.S., you basically have to decide between your career and your baby on your way down the hospital elevator.

Whatever you decide, try to make that decision well in advance of the due date. (Let's not forget that due dates are just fun guesses.) Have a candid talk with your partner in which you make clear that the goal is for you to minimize stress, maximize your ability to have quality time with your baby (and if staying home all the time would drive you nuts, that's not actually quality time) and to keep your finances in relatively stable condition. Don't assume what he wants, and **he shouldn't assume you'd want to quit and stay at home.**

For our relationship, that meant that I, at times, took freelance jobs to help cover daycare costs. It meant working the occasional night or weekend, but it was worth it.

We valued having my wife home with the kids as much as we could afford. That meant that she had to leave her full-time career in a leadership role. While she would be the first to say she's not someone who loves working in an office, she does sometimes miss being around adults all day. On the other side, I miss the trips she gets to take with our children to the museum or to the park. Overall, it works for us, and even if we are two ships passing in the night, we know this isn't forever.

What's most important is knowing _your_ "must haves," both as a couple and as parents. Don't let a friend or family member pressure you into something you don't want to do. The two of you can figure it out. And sure, you can talk to others to get some ideas. After all, if there's one good thing to crowdsource, it's finding an awesome daycare. People who love theirs won't shut up about it, and people who had a bad experience will gladly complain.

One thing to be cautious of as you sort all of this out is family members who volunteer to watch your baby every day. That's great if they do! What you want to avoid, though, is someone doing it for a few weeks and realizing it's not for them. That leaves you in a situation where you're now back at work with no childcare provider and Thanksgiving is officially awkward from now until forever. Sure, it can work, but be extra sure your volunteer is prepared for it. Try a couple of four to five hour stretches to start and go from there.

Two things to consider when deciding about the daycare/work balance:

Don't assume, if one of you is the primary earner, that you are stuck. Don't assume the status quo is the best. If both of you work, maybe it makes sense for one of you to quit. Don't assume that just because more often it's the mom that stays home, that's what will be best for your family. Stay-at-home-dads are slowly becoming more prevalent. Go into your conversation with your partner only focused on what will work for *your family*, and don't let him guilt you into anything. This isn't 1950. You get to make a decision too.

Don't assume full-time daycare or an adjusted work schedule is off the table. There are a lot of flexible options out there. Maybe you can work from home some days or perhaps your boss can offer some other kind of flexibility. I've had bosses who've let me adjust my schedule so that we don't need a babysitter to take the kids for an hour until I can get home in the afternoons. That saves us hundreds of dollars a year. As I mentioned before, maybe your work has a dependent care savings account that can help you set aside pre-tax dollars to make daycare more affordable. Know the maternal and paternal leave policies in advance, and have a good talk with your respective bosses to ensure your exact job will be there when you get back (which, legally, they're required to hold for you, but, you know ... people can suck sometimes.)

That's why it pays to have this talk with plenty of time to think it through. Maybe the goal is to get yourselves in a good financial position so that you can start saving for your kid's college fund. Maybe it's having one of you there for all of the precious moments, and for those crocodile tear moments as well. Maybe breastfeeding is important and pumping doesn't seem realistic or practical. The bottom line is that you'll need time to figure out all of these things. At the very least, you probably need to do some budgeting and then really think about what's important.

What if he's the stay-at-home dad?

For starters, let me remind you that guys are always thinking about how to provide, even if they aren't a natural at it. So they might naturally be more freaked out about the finances, especially if they think your budget is about to have a hacksaw taken to it.

Let's imagine that your partner is the one staying home. Here's what one dad, Pat H., said to me about the prospect of a guy becoming a stay-at-home dad:

"Don't get caught up in owning lots of stuff and such. Focus on supporting your wife, raising your children, being a man."

That's a good way for a dad to look at it. It's a mindset shift for him. He's a provider but in a new fashion. He's not there to provide funding for everything you do, from paying the mortgage to financing trips to Target. He needs to know that you aren't going to be frustrated with him if money is tight; you can be frustrated with the situation, but that's different. Instead, he can be focused on supporting your family's well being. You can't go wrong with a man who provides for his family's whole self and not just their physical needs.

Another dad, Aaron G., emphasized how you have to be open to change because jobs and finances aren't always firm when a baby is involved:

"We never had predefined roles or expectations. We left it fluid and dependent on the circumstances."

There are pros and cons to everything. If you have to write it all down on a piece of paper full of charts and budgeted numbers, great. If it's just a few heartfelt conversations over wine, awesome. Just don't wait until the last day of maternity leave, OK?

I can't say what you should do. I can't say what will make you feel the happiest with the least amount of guilt or anxiety. While I know that you'll do your due diligence when it comes to childcare, you can never know for sure what will happen, and I know that can be very stressful.

What I *can* tell you is that your baby loves you already. You and your husband are going to do your best to provide for your family. I never uttered the phrase "provide for my family" until I became a dad, and now it's something that's central to who I am. As long as you think it through and accept that there are no perfect decisions, you're going to be OK.

You're always making the right decision when you make it with your family's well being in mind.

8

Romance: Oh yeah, that.

Ideally, you want 100% husband, 100% dad. Realistically, though ...

What does a "successful dad" look like to you?

I don't mean physically, although you're likely envisioning flannel and a beard.

I mean, what are the markers of successful fatherhood? In order for you to deem your partner "a success," what would he be doing, saying and achieving?

You may have a good idea of what a successful mom looks like.

Perhaps, from your perspective, a great mom:

- Has a full slate of brain-building activities ready to hand her children at a moment's notice;
- Feeds her kids nothing but organic, homemade snacks and meals;

- Always finds time for the gym (and it shows) while maintaining a healthy libido;
- Is always put together, especially when she's out in public — at least wearing makeup and real pants;
- Finds time to see her friends, write thank-you notes and keep a career or volunteer work going;
- Basically, is Michelle Obama or Joanna Gaines.

I'm not saying any of that is feasible, especially if you happen to have several kids. But am I wrong? Wouldn't most moms, if not all parents, say "If I could do that, I'd be crushing it!"

But then you'd laugh and say "Hahaha hell no. That's not happening," and you'd go back to your sweatpants and fast food and Netflix or whatever else gets you through. #nojudgment

That's not settling. That's surviving. You're grinding through those early days second-guessing yourself, downplaying the victories and amplifying the little mistakes.

Doing what you can to provide the best life possible for your baby often involves compromise. It's called balance. You're still a great mom; the fact that you're reading a book like this means that you're obviously invested in giving your baby the best possible life.

Meanwhile, in the midst of all that parenting craziness, you're also somehow trying to be a loving, attentive and romantic spouse. (When foreplay turns into "Hey babe, I did the dishes and put the kids to bed.")

Maybe your guilt-driven mind tells you that tonight's the night to bust out your Victoria's Secret, but then your exhausted, drained and un-showered self convinces you that Victoria needs to keep that damn secret locked up tight.

Your mind tells you to plan an afternoon of crafts and activities so that you can feel like the mom you've always told yourself you'd be, but then your sleep-deprived self says "Screw it," as you turn on *Mickey Mouse Clubhouse* and collapse on the sofa. #seriouslynojudgementyoudoyou

Being an involved dad means juggling fatherhood and romance in a similarly impossible balancing act. More often than not, I get the feeling that I'm lacking in one or the other. Some days my brain is so overwhelmed, I just want to bury my face in my phone, and my wife is kind enough to gently remind me to put it away. Other days, I realize that I haven't once asked my wife how she's doing because I'm focused on work or whatever we have going on with the kids.

I promised you some insight into what a dad might be thinking as he's trying to fill these new and evolving roles. What I've realized is that the "winning" mentality guys grow up with can easily translate into fatherhood. For guys who want to be involved, we often end up trying to "win" fatherhood.

I want you to imagine a dad who's diving head first into fatherhood. On the surface, everything seems ideal! In fact, we just spent seven chapters talking about how important it is for dads to be involved, and yet, there are drawbacks if the pendulum swings too far in that direction.

Let's imagine what a "100% all-in" dad looks like.

That first night at home with the baby, he's anxious and exhausted but present, rocking your swaddled newborn between your breastfeeding or bottle sessions. He's in love with this baby, even after worrying for months about not having the connection with the pregnancy that you did.

Fatherhood suits him. He's posting photos nonstop and doing skin-to-skin like it's his J-O-B, cause, well, it is.

Weeks go by, and man, he's so tired that he could fall asleep standing up!

But he's also really embracing this whole fatherhood thing, from the late-night diaper changes to the bottle feeds to the doctor's appointments.

It is harder than either of you ever imagined, sure. Some days he's losing his mind over how to deal with it all, and by the time he gets home from work (or you do), a crying baby is almost too much to deal with, but he presses through and picks her up because he wants to take care of her, and who can resist that eventual baby giggle, anyway?

There's no way he can do everything his increasingly amazing wife does — you are suddenly a superhero to him as you juggle pumping/nursing/formula mixing/extra laundry/tracking down organic baby food recipes (gotta get at least perfect mom one bullet point done!).

However, he's confident that he's embracing fatherhood as the kind of dad he's always wanted to be.

It's the hardest role he has ever had, but damn it, he is DOING IT.

A typical day for your 100% dad type:

- He gets up for work, and by that I mean he gets up from a series of mini-naps in between soothing the baby so that you can get some rest after a long day of nursing or bottle feeding/spit up cleaning.
- He changes the baby's diaper, gives her a kiss on the forehead, hands her off while confirming his plans with you for the day and then heads out to work.
- He checks in on the baby all day, oohing at photos and talking about her with coworkers, because he's so proud to be a dad.

- He gets home, tired, sure, but so are you. He's ready to parent with a tag-team approach.
- He changes a diaper and takes the screaming baby out for a car ride to calm her down. He also gets some errands done while he's at it. The sight of a dad and baby out together on their own undoubtedly elicits kind remarks from strangers (who would never say the same to you, naturally).
- Victorious at calming her down, and with you recharged, he returns home for dinner, which at this point is mostly a revolving door of one person eating and the other person feeding the baby. Phew.
- Almost done for the day, so after another diaper change and a new outfit, he spends the last hour of the night making multiple attempts to put your "sleeping" daughter into her crib between nursing sessions. Eventually, it works, and he passes out beside you. He did it! He supported the family and took care of the baby's needs as much as possible. Other moms are jealous. You won the husband lottery!

There's just one ingredient missing from that "perfect" dad day.

Romance.

Marriage is, no doubt, about more than just romance. The same goes if you're in a long-term relationship, but for the sake of argument, I'll refer to marriage.

Raising kids can easily become the sphere around which the marriage orbits, and as I've pointed out, part of a thriving marriage means sharing those duties so that you feel supported. *But it's not everything.*

Confession time: Give or take a twin and/or a toddler, I've just described a day that I've had before. Shit, am I narcissistic?

Am I tooting my own fatherhood horn, so to speak? Well, yeah, Andy, you asshole, but still, at least this time, I'm using myself as an example of what *not* to do because it's majorly lacking in one area. The routine I've just described isn't too far off from the best of my dad days.

I confess that I sometimes go into "full dad mode" and save all my mental and emotional energy for the little ones and for what it takes to support my family.

Except where does that leave time for nurturing a marriage?

My wife is the most nurturing, caring and loving mother my kids could ever ask for. I'm sorry Michelle Obama, but she's got you beat.

If you know my wife, you may be nodding along. She's an incredible human being who only slightly rolls her eyes at my dad jokes. The fact that I even had time to write this book is due to her. Not only has she given me actual time to write, but she's given me the mental space to write the book in my head by helping me process my thoughts all the time.

Day after day, she makes sure our kids' needs are met, even when that most certainly means she's worse for the wear (tandem nursing twins should be an Olympic sport). On top of that, she's constantly supporting me, from my career to my instablog to doing little things like making me an entire sheet of cookies that I most certainly did *not* eat all of in the space of about 12 hours. Ahem.

On top of all of that, she teaches college classes and spin classes. No, you can't have her. I have dibs. Vow dibs.

We're best friends and I love her more every day, which means tomorrow I'm going to love her like you wouldn't believe, considering the fact that today I love her completely. That's not mushy word vomit. That's the truth, and there's no reason to water it down.

Even with all that, sometimes without intending to, she gets B-team Andy compared to the A-team Andy that my kids get.

That's the rub. **The goal isn't to have your partner become a dad who is so consumed with taking care of your baby and supporting the family that he neglects your needs.**

That's not an all-star caliber performance. That's an Instagram Father performance: He has all of the outward appearances of dominating the dad thing, but it's just surface level, like someone who only posts photos of themselves with six different filters and in ideal lighting against a gorgeous, urban wall mural. Which is 81% of Instagram. (That's not a made-up statistic. Yes it is, as are 73% of all statistics.)

For me, some days I feel like a 100% dad, 0% husband.

I try to be the best husband I can be. We're seven years in. We've gone through job changes and house changes and the birth of three kids and, somehow, we're still golden. If we weren't, I wouldn't be writing this!

But sometimes, man, I suck. In the pursuit of becoming a 100% dad — the guy who's always there for his kids, who supports them and nurtures them and loves them, who's doing what everyone thinks a great dad should do — it's easy to act and feel like a 0% husband.

You can't pour every ounce of energy and focus into one aspect of your life and expect the other areas to be just fine, thanks. And when there's a baby around, the natural tendency is to put everything into the baby.

"The baby needs all of our attention. It will be fine to not go on a date for awhile/skip an anniversary celebration/just turn on Netflix and go to bed."

Some days? Sure, that's fine. Newborns need a lot of attention! But you'd both be wise to make sure it doesn't become a habit where one day you realize you're just two adults who happen to take care of the same baby together. That's why we must be intentional, because we all know how easily a day can snowball.

Weeks shouldn't go by without him showing affection, for instance. If you're instigating *every* intimate moment, that's a red flag! I'm not just talking in the bedroom. I mean hugs and kisses and hand-holding. All of it. You need to feel affection. You're a woman, not "just a mom." Does this already sound like something you've heard one too many friends bemoan?

Also, you shouldn't always have to cough loudly to get him to realize he hasn't asked about your day. Not asked about the baby. Asked about YOU.

Directly tell him this. Don't hint at it.

Tell him "Although I appreciate how much you love our daughter, it's tough for me when days go by and you don't talk to me about anything other than the baby. Can you sometimes ask what else is going on? I'd love to talk about adult stuff too!"

It's all a balancing act. Don't let your drive to be great parents throw your balance out of whack. Something has to give from week to week.

The tricky thing is that as a society, we're all begging for guys to become more involved in parenting, so the feedback he'll receive when he's all in will provide never-ending positive reinforcement. If friends and strangers are constantly telling him that he's perfect, it makes it tough for him to consider that he may be falling short in other areas. No one will ask him "Are you still taking your wife out on dates?"

Let's look at the whole picture.

That "Perfect Dad Day" description, now with 0% romantic partner context:

- He gets up for work, and by that I mean he gets up from a series of mini-naps in between soothing the baby so that you can get some rest after a long day of nursing or bottle feeding/spit up cleaning. *In a way, a gesture of romance! So that's a good move. Marriage/dating evolves with kids; romance changes too. Downside: Now he's exhausted because he's being too proud to admit that he needs some sleep, which means it's tougher for him to handle stress, i.e. to not be abrupt or terse.*

- He changes the baby's diaper, gives her a kiss on the forehead, hands her off while confirming his plans with you for the day and then heads out to work. *He's so caught up in the baby stuff that he forgets to kiss you goodbye or ask how you're doing.*

- He checks in on the baby all day, oohing at photos and talking about her with coworkers, because he's so proud to be a dad. *Years ago, checking in meant sending little love notes (Or maybe some sexts? Ooh la la!). Checking in on the baby is great, but it's too easy to make that the only thing you discuss. You're more than a mom, so it's not good to reduce you to just that.*

- He gets home, tired, sure, but so are you. *He's instantly focused on the baby's needs. Did he remember to give you a hug or talk about things other than the baby? Damn it, forgot. And on top of that, he snapped at you when you asked him to do something. You weren't being unreasonable, but you aren't getting his best effort and he doesn't think it through before he says something. Real smooth, dude.*

- He changes a diaper and takes the screaming baby out for a car ride to calm her down. He also gets some errands done while he's at it. *That free time after work used to go to spending quality time together with you, even if that meant doing errands together. It still could on some days if he found a babysitter or a family member to watch your son for 30 minutes (with the important note that he needs to be the one to find a sitter, or it will just be another chore that falls to you). Instead, he takes the baby on his own, because "perfect dads" take care of the baby on their own. No one is going to chide him for spending time with his kid. Unless week after week, he's forgoing spending a date night with his wife. He figures he can always do it later. Dummy.*

- Victorious at calming the baby down, and with you recharged, he returns home for dinner, which at this point is mostly one person eating and the other person feeding the baby. *Phew. As a 100% romantic partner, he would have maybe found new recipes for you to enjoy or picked up your favorite takeout or taken time to laugh together about some goofy thing you did. But on a 0% husband day, focusing all of his energy on being a dad means dinner time is just an exercise in eating.*

- Almost done for the day, so after another diaper change and a new outfit, he spends the last hour of the night making multiple attempts to put your "sleeping" daughter into her crib between nursing sessions. Eventually, it works, and he passes out beside you. *If he's lucky on a 0% romantic partner day, he makes sure to kiss you before he goes to bed. You're exhausted too, but it sure would be nice if you had a little cuddling!*

Yikes. Not quite as dreamy, is it?

Find the balance of parenting and romance.

"Well NOW what am I supposed to do? Forget my kid? Tell my wife tough luck?" he wonders, scratching his head as you share this book with him.

What he needs to do is find the balance and be intentional to not let a day or two of intense focus on one area mean that he falls into a pattern of neglect for another. He doesn't have to try to be perfect. And you don't expect him to be. Together, you find a happy medium where he's holding up his end of the parenting bargain without making you feel like a zero on the priority scale.

Tell him he doesn't need to "win parenting." You love his enthusiasm, I'm sure. Lovingly help him see when he needs help getting into a sustainable, balanced groove. It's really hard to do!

I can tell you right now, continuing a powerful, loving relationship with your partner is probably one of the least focused on aspects of being a parent of a newborn. You can read book after book about parenting a newborn and not find a single word about doing all of that while also maintaining a great relationship.

It's as if we're all so obsessed with parenting that we forget what got us into this in the first place — wanting to build something meaningful with someone whom we love. If you're reading this book, you're the kind of person who wants great things for your relationship; why else read something that explicitly says it's trying to help you help someone else?

You can't let the baby define you, and you can't let the baby

define the way you value your partner.

There's no perfect solution. It's not feasible to think every day either of you can be everything to everyone, that he'll always do crazy romantic things for you while also teaching your kid to play guitar and coaching the soccer team and booking an anniversary dinner. Or that you'll read books to your baby for hours and then have a candlelit dinner ready followed by sexy lingerie (because, let's be honest, you're going to be rocking a nursing bra like it's a second skin).

Romance changes for parents, and that's OK. I once saw a mom write this to her husband on PigandDac.com, and it stuck with me: "For every dirty diaper you change, every hour you put in at work, every time you get up in the middle of the night ... I'm going to remember that these are the romantic gestures right now. This is what real love looks like."

Be honest with him if you feel neglected. If it's coming from a place of wanting more one-on-one attention, that's a compliment to him. That means you desire him, love him and want him. Um, yes please! He may be going into fatherhood with so much gusto that he kind of forgets he has more than one role; guys are already predisposed to be obsessive when we're tackling a new activity.

Tell him you want to choose a few hours each week that are just for the two of you. Put it on your calendar. Stick with it, even when you're too tired. Get a sitter or call in that favor. It's important.

Also, don't overthink the intimacy aspect! Any intimacy expert will say over and over that it's not all about sex. Taking a nap together is still intimate, as is giving each other a long kiss or having a deep conversation or sharing a meal.

It's not about putting pressure on the two of you. It's about remembering that parenting is WAY easier if you feel like you're on the same page as your partner. Some days, you're not even going to feel like you're in the same book. That happens. But by making it a priority to invest time together, you're actually being better parents.

Once we got into the toddler stage with our oldest, my wife and I laughed over how we ever thought having one tiny baby was difficult and how we didn't leave the house for months because of him. We could have gotten out more, for sure.

The reality is that it's all context; it was overwhelming with one because we were learning everything on the fly. Otherwise, we would have gone out more and realized that it's OK to hire a babysitter and go on a date.

No one is served if you sacrifice yourselves and/or your marriage to parental martyrdom.

Now we're much better about going out. Man, does that feel good. Do we get to go out all the time? No, but we do have a shared hobby (improv comedy) that gives us a good reason to be together outside of the house doing adult things (like wearing real clothes and having conversations that don't involve the phrases "nap time" or "milestones"). We're never going to keep up with our friends who don't have kids, but then again, it's not a competition.

I tell dads all the time: She doesn't stop being your wife just because her title is now "mom."

The same goes for dads.

The goal isn't for him to be 100% romantic partner and 100% dad.

He'll burn out trying to please everyone.

Let's go for having him strive to be a 100% great guy.

How does that sound?

About being the "old you."

My wife was returning from a trip with a girlfriend. She had this huge smile on her face, her skin was glowing, and she was just so ... at peace.

As you come to learn with babies and toddlers around, "at peace" is an oxymoron. It's very difficult to be at peace when you're trying to figure out if the brown stuff on the carpet is chocolate or poop, and if you think you won't be sniffing the carpet, hahahahaha no, for real, you're going to be sniffing the carpet.

It's very difficult to be at peace when the baby has a slight fever, because it's nearly impossible to brush that off when you've heard too many horror stories of a fever turning into something else (even if we both know the fever is, indeed, just a fever.).

It's very difficult to be at peace when you never get to wear all those outfits you love, curl up with a book under a blanket or grab a drink after work like you used to. You can feel fulfilled! You can feel in love! You can feel like you were destined to be a mom! But at peace? Not likely, at least not at first.

Even so, there she was, looking like she figured out life's secrets. Truly, the secret was just getting away for an extended weekend.

"I feel like I got to be ... me," she said.

I knew exactly what she meant.

When you become a mom or a dad, you become Mom and Dad. I'm Elliott's Dad, Quinn's Dad, Hannah's Dad. I'm very sure that many people only know me as that, which is fine because I don't know their names either, and I will straight up kill you if you tell them that.

You might be used to having your role change.

At one point, you were you.

Then, maybe you became someone's fiancée. And then someone's wife. Or you became the director of something. Or a teacher. Or the person who always does the community theatre productions. Or the person who always writes thank-you cards the day after you receive a gift. Or the person who always spends hours doing research and therefore comes up with the perfect Christmas gift for everyone on your list. You were you. Not perfect. Not a finished product. But "You."

When you become a parent, it's unavoidable that your identity will change. Let me be clear. There are a million benefits to becoming Mom or Dad. I love that most people I know think of me as a dad. It's the thing I'm most proud of!

It doesn't mean that I'm *only* a dad, however, and you are not *only* a mom. Not even close!

It can feel that way, though. That's what my wife was getting at when she said she felt like she was the old Sara again. Because *that* Sara got to go off to places like New York City for fun weekend adventures full of shopping and new restaurants and nights out on the town. My wife flourishes in those situations! So, when she has the chance to do it, it can feel like she's staring at an alternate version of herself, like someone she used to know.

It's so very important that both of you find ways to give each other and yourselves *permission* to be all the different versions of you. You can't just be Mom 24/7! You need to go out with your girlfriends regularly *just because*. Not just once a year for someone's bachelorette weekend. Also, your husband doesn't get to make a big deal of it, like he's doing you a favor by watching the baby so you can go out and party. Nope. He's watching the baby because A) It's his damn baby and B) Being a great parent also means taking the time to take care of yourself so that you can come back to your children refreshed.

If you're going at it nonstop as Mom, you're going to hit a wall. Hard. Same for him, if he's doing a stay-at-home dad thing, for example. You need built-in "you" time.

The benefits are everywhere. You will feel more like a complete person if you can have conversations about something other than whether or not your baby has colic. You will feel sexier if you get to wear real pants with buttons. You will feel more relaxed if you get to spend a few hours *not* enslaved to a feeding schedule. (Side note: If you go out for dinner, remind yourself to chew slowly. You don't have to race to eat before the baby wakes up. This is shared from personal experience.)

I get so pissed at dads who act like they're doing the world a favor by letting a mom go out. Holy shit, you suck, man.

That mentality is entitled, bratty and childish. I'm a very involved dad, and I still think about my kids a fraction as much as my wife thinks about them. She is an amazing human being, to say the least. She's constantly planning activities, meals, summer camp schedules, as well as a hundred other things, all the time, every day. Because, honestly, someone has to, and often that's the mom. She *needs* the breaks as often as I can make them happen, whether it's taking a night out or going to Target alone for a little while.

What if you and your husband are even in the childcare duties? That should make it even easier to find breaks. Make it a point to find time in your calendar for each of you to go out by yourself with no particular errand in mind. (Don't tell him, "You can have Sunday morning, and while you're out, I need
_____." That's not a break.)

When the time for these breaks comes up, stick to them, even if the baby is being a bit cranky or you're both tired. There's always a reason. Anyone can find time to get a break when things are swell. But the real breaks are needed after a long night or a hard day of nursing or an afternoon in which you just cannot figure out what this baby WANTS, for goodness sake!

Maybe you sign up for the painting class you've always wanted to try. Or he bowls every Sunday afternoon. Or you have friends over every other Friday night, and he puts the baby down and is on baby duty until they leave.

Everyone focuses on the baby early on. Who will change the diaper? Who's taking the baby to the doctor's appointment? Who's doing daycare pickup? The list goes on, and it doesn't stop when they're toddlers. It only gets busier. You'll never run out of things to worry about or things to do for your kid, so there will never come a time when you say, "Everything is done! Now it's time for me!"

Make time for you. Make sure he's making time for him. The baby will still be there. Your parents or a friend or an awesome babysitter can watch her for a few hours.

She will be OK. I promise.

You're a mom. He's a dad. But you're still you as long as you take the time to remind yourself of that.

9

You're not "just a mom."

A dad can't treat you like you ceased being a woman with individual needs just because you happened to have his kid.

There's a photo of my wife, Sara, and me from years ago posing with several of her cousins and immediate family.

I distinctly remember the day we took that photo, because it's the day I became a vegetarian. We had only recently started dating. My wife had long been a vegetarian, and I was curious about it so I did what I always do in these situations and researched the hell out of it. On the plane ride to Florida to meet several members of her family, I made the decision. I was no longer eating meat. (It's been a number of years, and the last piece of meat I ate was a Wendy's cheeseburger at the airport before we took that flight. Of course, I had no idea how to be a vegetarian and my first meal was basically all potato-based!)

My wife is gorgeous in the photo, wearing a sunny yellow dress and her signature smile. She always makes a priority of traveling and having experiences rather than focus on getting "things." (Although she is quite fine with getting a pair of Kate Spade sunglasses or a gift card to Sephora, thank you.) In fact, in the time before we had kids, we traveled to Mexico, Greece, Florida, New York City, and other destinations.

In the Florida photo, we both look less tired than we often do now; kids single-handedly created the anti-fatigue face mask market. This was before we had kids. In fact, in the years since, one of those cousins got engaged, and her brother and our future sister-in-law got married and had two sons. We, of course, got married and had three kids. So much has changed. I have more gray hair. My wife has less opportunity to put a dress on (although when she does ... wow).

That photo shows off two people who were defined as "boyfriend" and "girlfriend." At the time, I was a newspaper reporter, and she worked in higher education, so you could define us by that, too. Or maybe "friend." "Family member." "Excellent party thrower."

We were Andy and Sara then. We are Andy and Sara now. But the identifier has changed.

When you have kids, your entire identity seems to come down to one word. "Mom" or "Dad." Your small talk ends up being about your kids. When you see someone you haven't in some time, you being a mom or dad will probably be the first thing they bring up. Your social functions end up revolving around fitting in time to catch up with friends while you simultaneously breastfeed or keep an eye on an infant crawling across the floor. You make mom friends/dad friends whom you only really know as "So and so's mom." (One day, you really should ask for their first name but we both know you're too far down that road.)

And you know what? I don't mind it. I feel like I offer a lot in a lot of different ways. I'm an improv comedian, a speaker, a marketing professional, a friend, a husband, a brother, and now, an author. But most people know me as a dad first, perhaps because I end up talking about my kids in most any situation. It would be annoying if I thought that people think less of me because of thinking of me as one thing, but damn, being a dad is a pretty great thing to be known for out of all the options. It's where I have the biggest impact. It's what I spend the most time trying to improve.

What I can't do and won't do, though, is think of my wife in the same capacity.

She's my wife. My partner. The love of my life.

Is she still a mom, through-and-through? You bet your bake sale she is. She volunteered for the PTO at my son's elementary school before he even started class!

But dads need to be careful. They can't start thinking of you less and less as their romantic partner. You're getting enough of that from everyone else!

It's a trap that's easy to fall into, as he'll spend so much time around you where you're both talking about the baby. Instead of having a chance to be flirty with you at a party, you're both skipping the party and staying up late dealing with your baby's fever. The dressing up events turn into sweats and staying in. The thoughtful gestures he perhaps did to woo you seem to fade away because guys all get in such a provider mode that the idea of doing stuff just for you, the grown woman with her own needs, seems like a distant memory. A friend told me of all things as a new mom she wishes her husband did differently, talking about things other than the baby was right at the top of the list.

111

What does that mean for a dad to not put his partner in "the mom trap"?

It means your partner shouldn't skip date nights.

My wife and I regret how much we stayed in when we only had one baby around. Hindsight is 20/20, sure, so after having twins, the idea of only one baby around seems like a tropical vacation. At the time, we really stressed about going out. We took him out with us to restaurants some, and we'd get the occasional babysitter so we could go to an event.

But we didn't make a priority of going on dates. Part of that was that we were so very, very tired that the date night might have been walking to our SUV and falling asleep in the driveway. But, hey, date! Part of that, though, is that I think we were a little worried (or at least I was) that we wouldn't be perceived as being dedicated if we took time for ourselves. Does that make sense? As if people would see a pic of us on a romantic dinner on a non-anniversary occasion, and think "Yeah, but what about your baby?"

So dumb, Andy.

No one else is in the relationship but the two of you. No one else deals with the consequences of ignoring chances to nurture your relationship. You have to make the time, and you know what? Your baby will still be there when you get back.

Action step this week: Ask around for babysitters others trust, have them do a trial run for an hour so you can run to the store, and if all seems well, book them for the next Friday night. And have your partner take you out. Get dressed up. Eat a long, flavorful and enjoyable meal with forks and everything. Go out for a drink! Go dancing! Sing some bad karaoke!

Because if you're not going on dates and all you do is either work or take care of your kid ... aren't you just roommates? He has to keep in mind that you didn't stop wanting to go out just because you now have a kid. It just means there are more logistics to figure out. Logistic it up. Get outside.

It means he can't only offer you physical touch on his terms when he wants to fool around.

I can't count the number of times I've seen on dad message boards — yes, they exist, and yes, your partner should find a dad Facebook group so he can have some emotional support and community — a post from a dad who is bemoaning the lack of sex he and his wife are having.

I am not a sex therapist. I'm not even going to attempt to figure out what's an appropriate frequency, especially with a baby or toddler around; I think you know when it's enough and you definitely know when it's not enough.

But what I do know is that he can't treat you like a sex robot. He can't ask you to flip the switch when he's ready for naked time, which, let's face it, is how guys are programmed to act. "Hey babe, when you're done feeding the baby, throw on something sexy and seduce me. Thanks."

Guys can't think that moms are no longer sexual beings! That's how they start diverting their attention elsewhere, in small ways or big ways.

More importantly, he needs to keep up with what I am sure he was doing before you had a baby. Rubbing your shoulders, or kissing your neck, or holding your hand in the car, or any number of little touch points throughout the week that let him show you that he still desires you ... it's so important!

It may be physically impossible for so many reasons for you two to get busy, but that doesn't mean he should completely stop doing any other number of things to be intimate. Partners still whisper dirty things in the other person's ear. They grab each other's butts. They cuddle. If he's only viewing you as the mom of his kid because he's so mentally focused on parenting, all of that starts becoming a secondary priority, and it can't! One day, your kid will be grown and gone. Then what?

I'll be honest, sometimes my wife and I just make out. For no reason, and in completely random places. And then we go on with our day. It's hot and it's romantic and it doesn't require any huge time commitment or planning.

Grab a butt, dudes. Save a relationship. I want him to hold your hand when you're walking with the stroller (and grab his from time to time, too).

It means he needs to put effort into your relationship like he did before the baby arrived, because you're still *in* a relationship.

I've always been a romantic gesture guy. In some cases, this was not a good approach. "Try hard" may have been my unofficial motto growing up. I remember the time in high school I had a crush on a girl I met over the summer who lived across the state. We talked back and forth a lot on AOL Instant Messenger (natch), and I thought what would seal the deal would be a grand gesture to show my admiration.

I got in my car with some flowers and drove two hours to her house, unannounced, as I knew in my head that she would surely see that I thought so highly of her I'd drop everything to see her in person.

What followed was an extremely awkward "Um, why are you here?" greeting and a couple hours of awkward hanging out by a girl who was too kind to send me packing right away, and I was too naive to realize this wasn't working. Coincidentally, we didn't talk much after that and we did not, as I figured we would at 17, get married.

The thing is, it can be so much easier to make an effort to either start or maintain a romantic relationship before you have a baby around for the simple fact that you don't have your schedule revolve around diapers and feeding time and play dates. I could drive a couple hours because I didn't have anything preventing me (and Jesus, I should have had something preventing me).

Maybe he used to get you flowers, or maybe he would send you a few texts throughout the day just because he missed you. Guys will really puff up like peacock to woo someone, so I'm guessing he could have done any number of things to impress you (and evidently, it worked!).

You are worth wooing every year. Yes, it would be unrealistic to think he could up keep that pace, but he needs to continue on some level approaching this like he needs to woo you. A long day with the baby seems a little more tolerable if he comes home with flowers. Or if he talks to you about topics other than the baby, just like he used to, because he's fascinated by who you are and being a mom isn't the only thing you are. Or if he gets a little flirty with you out of nowhere, just because. Honestly, when I catch myself having days in a row of not doing that with my wife, I feel off. She is worth wooing. And it helps us get back on track.

This doesn't mean he has to spend thousands of dollars, although, sure, go ahead if that's your thing! He can do so much by just reminding himself that you still have a relationship underneath all of those Puffs and high chairs and sippy cups. If you feel like he's doing nothing to maintain that, this is a fixable problem! He should act like he wants to be around *you*, the woman, and not just be going through life with you, the mother.

It means your kid should grow up and not think it's strange for mommy and daddy to cuddle or hold hands or kiss.

Our kids, at this point, have definitely seen us holding hands, giving each other a kiss just because, or taking a moment to say goodbye each morning rather than rushing out the door.

We say "I love you" all day, every day, and our kids also now say it to each other and to us all day, every day, because that's what they assume is what you do in a family.

If your son or daughter, as they get older, would be completely baffled if your partner hugged you or said "I love you, sweetie, how was your day?" then you're on the wrong track. Kids are great in this way; they soak up what they see, so if anyone asked them, "How does daddy treat mommy?" they aren't going to filter it. They'll say exactly what they've seen. If they have never seen you act like a couple, that's what they think being boyfriend/girlfriend or married is like.

Give them a good example. Tell your partner he's setting the example for his kid, and that you love how he's doing so much for you. Kids soak everything up. They notice *everything*, and it's unrealistic to think he can go on autopilot for a couple years and then all of a sudden turn into Mr. Marriage.

It means he has to think about what you need sometimes, and not just what the baby needs. Because the thing is, the baby needs you to feel whole, too.

Sometimes, it's about listening.

My wife loves one specific drink at Starbucks. In fact, it's just about the only thing I've ever seen her order in a drive-through.

It's a grande Emperor's Cloud Tea with half water and half steamed soy and then sugar-free vanilla.

Somehow, she's found that perfect combination, and when

she has her first sip, she practically goes "Ahhhhhhhh." It's adorable.

So I know that if I have the chance I will grab her that exact drink and bring it with me when I see her next. That tea is my way of saying "I was thinking about you, and I wanted to find a way to make you smile."

It works.

It's not a gesture tied to our kids (although, to be fair, sometimes she could use a tea *because* of the kids). It's not me offering to watch the kids for a night so she can have a girls' night, or cleaning out all the crumbs in the van, or taking the kids for a long walk so she can relax. I'll do those things, just as she does the same for me, but those are more about sharing parenting duties and understanding what the other person needs in that moment.

The tea? That's for my wife. The person I married. The woman I want to woo for the rest of my life. It's a little romantic gesture and it's not tied to what our kids need or what she as a mom needs.

There is plenty of time for that. Your guy would do well to find a way to regularly do stuff just for you! You'll both be all the better for it. Parenting when you're in a relationship can mean so much more than "How healthy and happy is the baby?"

How healthy and happy is your romantic relationship? That matters, too.

Even if it's been nearly a decade and three kids since my wife and I took that photo in Florida, I'd like to think that the guy I was back then and the dad I am now are still making a priority of making that beautiful redhead smile every single day. She's still the same woman, after all.

Check that.

She's even better.

10

What no one talks about when it comes to fatherhood.

Feeling feelings he may have never dealt with until now.

"Daddy, you have to be nice."

I can't pinpoint exactly what it was that inspired me to seek out a therapist, but that phrase may have been one of the triggers.

Because I *wasn't* being nice.

I wasn't being a good dad.

I had never gone to a therapist before. I hadn't ever really felt like I needed one. I had it all handled. I was fine. "Fine, thanks for asking."

Until I wasn't.

Until I was punching walls, literally, and banging my head against the wall, metaphorically, and losing my temper, regrettably.

I was the father of three adorable, healthy, happy kids (at this point, all early toddler age), and I felt angry all the time.

While up to this point I've written about everything I've learned that worked for me in early parenthood, I've also been intentionally upfront with you. It's not just about signing up for the right class, making sure the dad handles his share of diapers or making time for each other. There's a mental side that dads (and moms) can go through that I think we too often hold inside. So here goes.

It turns out that it's not a good idea to bottle up all of your feelings and smile through gritted teeth. I'm pretty sure that's what homicidal maniacs do, in fact. But, unfortunately, it's the go-to approach for guys. Think about it. How often does your partner truly open up about his emotions and talk about what's eating at him? It's more likely you see him "in a mood" and just leave him alone, or he mumbles something about needing to go watch a game or whatever else will allow him to avoid what's gnawing at him. Typically, we're terrible at expressing emotion. At least expressing those emotions that we don't think will directly lead to us getting lucky.

One autumn, as we were deep in the throes of toddlerhood, I felt out-of-body. I had been a happy-go-lucky guy — and still, on most days at work and even at home, that's how I came across — but now that guy was slamming doors hard enough to make the house shake.

The guy who, at certain times when parenting alone, would shout "DAMN IT!" at the ceiling because of a *slight* inconvenience created by this toddler or that one. Who would clench his fingers before holding his kid's hand because he was trying to release anger like a kettle releasing steam.

Things had steamrolled. And they could for your partner too. I can't count how many dads I know who felt overwhelmed by the whole becoming-a-father experience. And moms too, in all fairness. Becoming a parent will reveal a lot about you, and you might not like what it brings to the surface.

So when my daughter told me that I wasn't "being nice," she was correct. Brutally, mortifyingly, correct.

I was doing all the "right" things in fatherhood but was, time and time again, failing at the core thing — being kind to the people in my home. Slowly, and then all at once, I became someone I didn't recognize. I didn't feel happy-go-lucky. I didn't feel like smiling.

Not because anything in my life had gotten worse in the prior year. In fact, I had an embarrassment of riches. What did I have to complain about? I had a beautiful, thoughtful wife, healthy kids, a nice house and a steady job. Two dogs … OK, the dogs drive me crazy, but that's because they think any wafting breeze is a potential threat that must be barked at with the veracity of a velociraptor defending its young. Still, a lot to be thankful for.

That made it all the more strange that I couldn't get a grip on myself. I was becoming a pessimistic, sometimes angry guy for no specific reason. But that's the thing: Anger isn't so easily tied to what you have or what you don't have. It's often about your *ability to process emotions*.

Parenting, for some people, is a pressure cooker. You may have been able to handle certain emotions in the past but find yourself needing to find entirely new ways to deal with the specific pressures related to parenting. The inability to cope can hit you before you realize it.

One time, I was so mad — so unbelievably, white-knuckled mad — while watching my twin one-year-old girls and three-year-old son, that I slammed a door in the house so hard I could feel the house reverberate. It was as though the house had shuddered at my outlandish and petulant behavior. I was being an asshole.

Another time, I threw a water bottle across the room at the wall because my son had, you know, asked for water a few times in a row. In that moment, he, like me, couldn't figure out why I had done that or how it had solved anything. Or I'd scream WHAT THE FUCK at the top of my lungs to no one because I had. Just. Had. It. It was like I was stepping outside myself, and even as it happened, I could hear a part of me saying "What is your deal?"

It wasn't me. But it very much was. You are who you are in that moment, and I wasn't being a nice or pleasant person, let alone a loving dad.

I was angry sometimes as soon as I woke up. Not angry like I wanted to lash out. More like I had a tense feeling in my chest like a branch pulled to its limits that was about to snap back.

Some days, everything could fall apart and I'd laugh and push through it and I'd be fully aware that this is just the stage of life I'm in; not a lot of control and an endless adventure. It wouldn't bother me much at all, and it wouldn't even be a big deal if the kids had a rough day. I'd be fine. No worries.

The next day, a slightly extended bed time full of babies popping back up or my son refusing to go to sleep would make me want to punch a hole in the wall.

Let me be clear right away: This is an internal anger thing, not about any kind of violent behavior toward my kids. I understand if you were startled reading any of that and were wondering otherwise because so rarely do any of us like to admit we have anything less than a glowing experience with our kids. *(If your partner has shown any signs of anything remotely related to violent behavior, please get professional help right away.)*

No doubt, I was dealing with some real stuff, and I'd spend

hours talking to my wife about it. She was as understanding and patient as ever, even as we were both wondering what had happened to the old me. I didn't want to keep going down that road. Already, I had heard my son mention a few times "daddy getting mad," and I knew exactly what he meant. That was enough.

I took a lot of time off from writing about fatherhood because I felt fake, for one, and also like I couldn't possibly weigh in on anything when I couldn't even handle myself.

Sure, I knew parenting hacks like you have to be strict about nap time, that you have to have a good understanding of swaddling, or that a loud sound machine is a life saver. And that any dad (or mom) could be all the better for having that info.

But I didn't believe in myself anymore. It's not that my heart wasn't in it — I hadn't stopped really valuing being an involved dad and helping new dads get quickly up to speed on everything they were about to experience. I was still just as active as ever otherwise.

It's that I was feeling hollow. That anything I would write needed a big, fat asterisk such as "*By the way, although I totally think this tip will help, I also yelled about a bath toy being wet today so take it with a grain of salt.*"

What makes a good dad? What makes a bad dad?

I kept wondering that. I wonder if your partner will, too.

I wondered how many dads were dealing with what I was dealing with, like they could show up for all the events and do all the bath times and read all the books and still have a side of them that was just fucking failing.

There's science behind this, too. A 2014 study published

in *Pediatrics* drew a lot of attention after researchers tracked about 10,000 men over the course of two decades. **Compared to guys who don't have children, men living with children ages newborn to five years old saw a 68% increase in depression symptoms.** Being a dad of a baby, it appears, can make you more likely to experience depression.

When we think about people becoming parents, I don't think there's a tendency to think, "I wonder if the dad may struggle during this new chapter of life"... and yet maybe we should.

Complicating matters is that men aren't talking about how they are feeling. Think of this: **Only 19% of men felt comfortable talking to others about their problems**, according to a 2017 study released by UK mental health organization Samaritans. It commissioned research about social attitudes around talking about mental health.

"This is despite the majority of male respondents saying they were happy to listen to other people who were finding life tough," wrote Samaritans CEO Ruth Sutherland in a post for the *Telegraph.*

So guys are aware and empathetic about other people struggling; they may be perfectly helpful at listening to you work through potential issues. But if you noticed he's struggling, all of a sudden he's a vault and you don't have the passcode.

When I first put it out there that I was dealing with this, dozens of parents reached out. Some of them left public messages of support. Even more sent me private messages with a simple and powerful theme: I do that, too. I've shouted. I've thrown a water bottle. I've been mean and regretted it. I've done all the things. Moms. Dads. People with fancy jobs. Stay-at-home parents. All kinds.

It was like they were relieved somebody they knew was in

the same boat, like it gave them the A-OK to raise their hand. In a way, their confessions warmed my heart. We're in this together! We share the same struggles! It also made me sad, because that meant I had friends and acquaintances who were privately not doing well and didn't feel like they could talk about it.

I am positive you know someone who isn't doing as well as they are letting on.

Moms and dads told me they couldn't believe how frustrated they'd get with their kids. They never pictured themselves being "that parent," and they were struggling to get better. They had yelled for no reason, or threw something in a vain attempt to regain control.

So if you or your partner start feeling like you're going down this path, do not feel like you're alone. I couldn't believe some of the people who reached out, people who I never would have guessed had dealt with anger like that. Nobody is immune. Parenting is hard.

My kids, who in the time since that period have grown into the most adorable, funny, sweet, exuberant kids you can ask for, deserved a better me.

Some days I could give that to them (even throughout all of this, I still had many fun, memorable days). And some days, my son would remind me that I needed to be nice because I had accidentally gripped his shoulder too hard with my tense hand as I was trying to do a delicate balance of working through a mental rage while dealing with the insanity of toddler reasoning (hint: there is none). Truly, the frustration toiling inside again and again was physically expressing itself in my grip.

I had to take a second to cool off and count 1, 2, 3, 4 like I was Daniel Freaking Tiger getting told he wouldn't get to ride

Trolley that day. Even now, I have to check myself, as evidently I channel frustration through my arms and hands. My wife is helpful in reminding me, too. You can't assume you've got it under control.

How I "pushed through." I got help.

I spoke with a therapist for the first time ever. And again. And again. And again.

I had no idea what was expected or what it would accomplish, but I knew I couldn't keep doing the same thing and assuming the results would be better.

My wife, who just wanted me to be happy and had already done what she could to get me some down time, agreed it would help to have me talk things out, as I had a tough time even explaining to her exactly what I was feeling. ("I just feel angry all the time and I don't know why," I remember telling her, which, considering I have so many wonderful aspects to my life, continued to make no sense on the surface.)

My therapist listened intently as I talked and talked, which, as I discovered, was the very best aspect of the sessions. How often do you get to just talk and not have someone try to give you a quick solution or interrupt or judge you? That's therapy.

She didn't try to justify things. Instead, she pointed out what should have been more obvious: that getting less than four hours of sleep a night for three years + having a daughter who almost died + having twins + regular work and life stress had pushed me to the breaking point. People handle that different ways. In my case, the extreme mental and physical exhaustion had manifested in bouts of anger, which was just stuff bubbling to the surface; really, it points to mild depression, she said. And

I ignored it for too long, thinking I could just ride it out until things got better ... except that's not how it works.

I had gotten to the point that, even if most people thought I was handling things well (It's amazing what we all do to have the outside world think we've got our shit together, right?), I couldn't really do it anymore. My kids needed me to have it together, and at that point, I couldn't deliver, and in some cases I just fell apart.

Realizing there was something deeper there than just a rough patch or "typical parent stuff" made it real, which helped me come to grips with it. It also was by no stretch an excuse. Just a reality. And one I needed to figure out for my sake, for my family's sake, and more. A rough patch shouldn't last for weeks and months on end. Anybody can have a moment of anger after a few bad days. If you're finding again and again that the anger doesn't have any real, tangible source, that's a warning sign.

While I worked through things, I laid low. I waited for answers, for some kind of breakthrough. I wanted to start to make changes to do something about it. Somehow.

I can't tell you what exactly helped snap me out of it. I'll never be entirely snapped, I suppose; you don't climb out of this quickly when it was such a long spiraling process to get down, and part of it is just core to my personality and how my mind approaches the world.

But I can tell you that every day now in the years since, I haven't been waking up angry. I don't get as easily frustrated. I am appreciating little victories more. I don't still feel "hollow." I'm enjoying things more, for sure.

Some of that is just the basic reality of the kids sleeping better, where adding just one hour more of sleep a night makes a huge difference. Our kids mostly sleep through the night and they also can play on their own more, and that means I get more space. That's no small thing.

Some of that is using techniques to take a mental step back when I feel that old feeling. Like stepping out of a room for a minute if I need to. Like making a bigger priority out of taking care of myself or being vocal about needing some time. Like being more aware of what kind of dad I wanted my kids to have, and knowing under no circumstance would that involve my son feeling the urge to say "you have to be nice." Those little victories add up.

One core thing that had bothered me? I had a big problem with not feeling like I was ever getting things done. I'm a "get stuff done" guy. It's part of how I identify and feel good about myself. So when I have months and years go by where I'd constantly be thinking "How come I never ever can get everything done?" even if it was just stuff around the house, it hurt. No joke.

What changes that?

It's something I want your partner to write down, especially if he's a guy who loves a weekend project or who seems restless if he's not checking things off a list. As my therapist told me, "Being a parent is a check off the list, too." Being a parent is an actual accomplishment, in and of itself. It doesn't need an addendum. It doesn't need a qualifier.

Being a dad IS the checklist. Being a mom IS the checklist.

That's an entirely different mindset. I am guessing if you've been nodding along this whole time, maybe it's something that can help you, too. But I'd say for men, it may be especially true that he'll have a tough time finding a balance now that he has a new priority entering his life, one that doesn't care what he has planned.

The shift focuses from "me" to "baby" in an instant.

It's not a stretch to say many guys don't seem take the transition to fatherhood—the move from "all me" to "all someone else"—all that well, at least not without some time and perspective. It was one thing when they went from bachelorhood to living with someone. At least that arrangement had some built-in benefits, and before long he didn't think anything of it.

Babies are not the same. This is not just a guy realizing he needs to pick up his laundry off the floor or put the toilet seat down or eat something that requires utensils and a real plate. This is a major, life-altering change. You already knew that. He might just be figuring it out.

He will realize he can't sleep in on Saturdays anymore (my wife and I like to alternate so that one of us gets to sleep in one day and then vice versa). Hell, he may not be able to "sleep in" on weekdays, either; 6 a.m. may seem like an extravagance. When my kids were babies, I could probably count on one hand how many times an alarm woke me up. Roosters wake people up less than babies—farms should just put a newborn outside their window, considering how babies can be real cock-a-doodle assholes at 4 a.m.

And many dads I know also realize they can't just kick back and play video games for a few hours anytime they want (I'm using video games as an example, but this could also be going out to a sports bar or working on his vintage car or any other favorite male pastime). Maybe that seems trivial to you. But for some guys, video games are part of their identity. They've been playing for 5, 10, maybe even 25 years, and although it's not true success by definition, it makes them feel like they are accomplishing something by reaching the next level, earning the next trophy, or helping their multiplayer team from across the globe storm the castle.

Sure, just like fantasy sports, it's not real ... but it's tangible. And now when they reach for the controller just as the baby goes down for a nap, and then the baby starts crying — again — and all of that fleeting hope for virtual relief goes up in smoke ... that's emotionally draining. I'm not saying it's worth crying over, but I get it! It sucks a little.

Guys need to know it can absolutely suck for moms, too. They need to know women are no less annoyed/impacted/stressed by a crying baby, and biologically speaking women are wired to respond to a crying baby. Seriously. A National Institute of Health study revealed that if you play the sound of a crying baby, women go on alert mode and men's brain activity remains unchanged. The report said that "earlier studies showed that women are more likely than men to feel sympathy when they hear an infant cry, and are more likely to want to care for the infant." That made sense centuries ago, I guess, if men were out hunting and women were caring for babies.

Not so much in the 21st century. Still, there can be a biological reason your partner doesn't snap to attention when your baby is crying, so please do remember that it isn't always just a case of him being uncaring. The dude literally isn't wired the same way. I mean, he needs to pay attention, but still.

With that in mind, both of you can be super stressed by all the pressures of taking care of a baby. In his case, keep in mind that he may feel like he's giving up a part of him that might seem inconsequential on the outside but matters to him more than he is letting on (and for more than superficial reasons).

Sex or a nap.

If they haven't already in those first few weeks, guys start to put it together soon enough that sex may be off the table for a while. Now, let's be clear. This isn't anyone's fault, as if women *owe* guys anything, as if he's got 10 punches on his husband membership card and wants to redeem one free session between the sheets. Good Lord. You pushed a watermelon out of your vagina. And if you had 15 minutes (or 3 minutes!), you'd rather sleep at this point.

But the reality is that he is presented with a new normal for a matter of months, if not more: Sex is now going to require, at the least, some planning. And as we all know, planning puts *everyone* in the mood. Haven't you seen all of those billboards on the Las Vegas Strip for Planning Shops? "Erotic Couples Scheduling Session. Who doesn't get physically aroused at booking a time to undress? Anyone? Hello? Why are you putting more clothes on?"

So he is thinking maybe it'll just take a few weeks or months for your body to remember what the hell it felt like before the bald squatter moved in. And then a few more weeks pass while you're desperately trying to get this baby to LATCH ALREADY WHAT THE HELL MAN. And then a few more weeks pass of your bed being used more as a temporary resting pod, let alone a marital bed.

That's if you even get to sleep in the same room! It's not a stretch to say there were many times the floor in my kids' rooms was basically my bed.

I used to have to take my son into the guest room so much each night — so my wife would get some semblance of sleep and then she'd get up early and let me go back to sleep — that he started calling the guest room "Daddy's Room" and our bedroom "Mommy's Room." I'm hoping he didn't tell that to our friends because that sounds like divorce.

All these weeks are passing. And the guy is starting to wonder what the new normal will be for intimacy, at least if you haven't had some conversations about it. Really, that's what can help more than anything. Just communication and expectations! Now that you've got a baby around, he needs to let you know if he's feeling lacking in that area (or vice versa, of course, if he never seems to be in the mood anymore).

That doesn't mean he "gets" anything other than a conversation. And that's a start.

In the meantime, there's a good chance your partner is trying to figure out his place in this new landscape. Those boobs? The ones he was such a fan of (probably especially when you were pregnant and got porn star boobs)? They belong to someone else. There's a baby on them All. The. Time. Or a pumping machine. When the Medela gets more nipple action than you, you know things are different. #WeirdAdCampaign

He needs to give it time, if that's what you need. So much is being asked of moms! And it'll balance out for dads. Scientifically, we know this because of younger brothers and sisters existing. Ahem.

Man cave? Time to come out of hibernation.

Then there's the man cave. I've never been a big fan of man caves, but that comes with the disclaimer that I drink Malibu Bay Breezes and it takes me half a year to grow a beard, so I'm not the picture of testosterone. Pre-baby, he'd spend hours in there, maybe with a few friends, watching March Madness or Sunday football or *Grey's Anatomy* (I do not presume what your partner watches. Maybe he has opinions about how Callie and Arizona ended things). No big deal.

But spending hours in there post-baby?

I'd hope he's not doing that, at least not with any regularity.

I get that if he's always been a huge MMA fan or watches his alma mater every Saturday, that might be his outlet and if he's otherwise crushing it 6.5 days a week and giving you some time to yourself, it stands to reason that it goes both ways.

That's ... an optimistic scenario.

Sure, in an ideal set-up, you both are taking a few hours each week to give the other person "me time." It's vital.

My wife made it a priority to take the kids every so often for a few hours for no other reason than to give me some personal space. She never makes a big deal of it, which I appreciate — it's not meant to be "Now you owe me!" — but it's also directly in response to me realizing through therapy that I need more of a break than I cared to admit. It's tough for me, for most men, for most *people*, to say "I need help."

I needed help. She's been excellent at making that a priority, and I do my best to give her time to herself, too.

But chances are you're not reading this because the ideal scenario is happening. Or you're a little worried it might not happen. Maybe you're thinking of a scenario in which he just wants to kick back with an ice cold chocolate daiquiri brewski and you're reminding him to put the baby down for a nap/clean the bottles/take out the Diaper Genie.

Is that nagging? NOPE.

It's not nagging to be balanced. You may be more aware of what needs to be done on a given day, so you're more likely to be on top of reminders.

My wife is clearly the one who sets the tone on what needs done and when, and thank God. She's fantastic at it, and I'm not, and I am very grateful she does it. I can't get upset with her because just when I was about to sit down, she mentions the breast milk bottles needed to be cleaned. (So many bottles.

Especially with twins. We should have bought stock in a baby bottle company.) If they needed to be cleaned, that can't wait! Pumping is on a schedule. In that same light, guys shouldn't hold it against moms who are just trying to keep things moving. That's unfair.

But the relationship dynamic can feel off-kilter when you go from a harmonious, let's-find-fun-things-to-do-every-weekend-and-cuddle-each-night types to two adults entirely focused on keeping this adorable, squishy, loud, messy bundle of joy alive and well. I've heard and read about way too many couples in that situation, with this "Who are we now?" feel to it all.

You may feel like you aren't yourself anymore. He doesn't either but he isn't expressing that. He's just grumbling and snapping and acting kinda like a dick. It'll seem like he's mad about not getting to do anything he used to do, and that you're somehow at fault ... but the truth is, he's feeling lost and unsettled, and he needs to come to grips with what his new life is offering.

That sounds all doom and gloom.

Like having a baby means no more fun. No more relaxing. No more sex. No more anything other than taking care of the baby.

It's not true.

It's so much better. Even as "control" feels so much worse.

Once he realizes what's possible, he'll be that much closer to becoming the kind of dad you've always wanted to be parenting with. And with it, an even better version of the guy you married.

This can happen with a simple check-in from time to time, asking how he's *really* doing and making it clear that saying he's drained or feeling overwhelmed is fine.

Sometimes, early on, I'd have this almost competitive game

in my head, without consciously trying to, of who would be more completely worn out between me and wife. It was dumb — there are no winners! And it didn't matter if one of us got less sleep. We were both beat. So I just started being more honest about what I was feeling, which in turn gave her more accurate info to work with; if I said I was really tired, she knew I wasn't saying it for effect but because it was my white flag of mercy waving.

Another conversation is finding out if he is frustrated about any changes that have happened since the baby arrived. It can almost feel like it's socially taboo to not love everything about the baby, as if doing so means you are a bad parent.

It's B.S.

It's Instagramming parenthood. It's not all smiles! If you're following people online who make you feel worse as a parent, stop it. There's no time for that.

In his head, he might feel like admitting he's bummed he can't do his favorite activity anymore is just off the table. Or maybe he's grumbling about it aloud because he (wrongly) assumes there's no real solution, and grumbling is the only outlet to his frustration.

If he gets the sense you acknowledge that he's upset and want to find some reasonable, common ground, it can mean the world. Seriously. It won't go unnoticed!

There's a real payoff to giving him the chance to let his guard down.

Pulling him out of a funk.

It is very, very, very important to realize that while I am sure you're going to see your partner crush it on the daily, it won't be the only version of new dad you'll see.

I would bet a full night's rest* that he's going to hit a wall. Or two. And maybe take awhile to get back up.

* Now that's a bet.

One of the reasons I wanted to write this book is because how much instant, powerful, and overwhelming feedback I got after sharing about my struggles with depression and anger as a dad. I didn't want anyone to feel like they were all alone in feeling like they were getting overwhelmed as a dad (or a mom). I didn't want them to think that they were the only ones to flip out at no one in particular while taking care of their baby because they just couldn't freaking deal anymore. It's really hard. I'm flawed at it, and I try my best, and I'm better at it now than I was.

Listen, I know you are smart. I know in your head you are thinking on some level that, sure, my partner is going to have a bad day sometimes and I bet I will too, and we'll get through it because we love our baby so much. Even if in a tiny corner of your brain late at night, you are whispering to yourself that maybe his bad days aren't going away. And then what?

You are heading into the biggest "Who knows" of life, after all. I don't care how many of your friends have had babies. Or how many baby nieces and nephews you've watched. Parenthood is an entirely different world. (And if someone tells you "Oh I'm a dog mom, I get it," punch them in the kidney.)

What I want you to keep in mind, even if it is just every so often in a quiet moment, **is that your husband is still your husband even in those really tough days**. And that he will need you to not lose sight of the fact he is trying his best. He'll need you to remember that when you're taking care of a baby, sometimes your best actually is NOT good enough, but you might just have to deal with it.

Babies are crazy town. My son was all kinds of adorable as an infant. His legs were just rolls upon rolls. He giggled like he was auditioning for a Gerber commercial. He would smile at anyone. He would take long naps on my chest. All of that was true. But he would also lose his mind at night sometimes for what seemed like no reason.

He would stay awake all night until 5 a.m., happy as can be, in what I assume was a CIA-sanctioned torturing experiment. And there were days when the smile I came home with would dissipate into a scowl by midnight. Even when I knew in my head this was both temporary and not anyone's fault, I felt victimized.

That's not a scenario for rational thinking.

When our daughters were added to the mix, everything got dialed up a to level 19 on a scale of 1 to Maury Povich. Two crying babies at once. Two girls who had different needs at different times. It exhausted my wife (who was nursing them both on top of everything else) when she watched them during the day in between teaching college classes. And when we switched at night, I would get drained like an iPhone with 5% battery.

I'm going to guess you don't hear about that side of parenting too much. Right? That side of things doesn't get mixed into natural conversation too often, as most of us tuck it away and pretend it doesn't exist, like some unwanted wedding gift you can't throw away. My wife and I like to joke that if any parent truly remembered what it was like taking care of a newborn, we'd all stick to one child.

My son was super colicky as a newborn, which is what doctors diagnose when they decide "Shit that sucks, good luck with that!" We had given up trying to get him to nap in his crib (Dumb!) and would spend days on end doing our best to have him take naps in the Pack 'n Play (which are designed by Satan and should be called Stay Put 'n Sob.) He would sleep, sure. For 15 minutes at a clip. Then he'd wake up screaming like he was getting paid per decibel.

I distinctly remember my wife and I taking turns falling asleep on the nearby couch in 15 minute increments — either she was nursing or I was using a syringe to squeeze milk into his mouth — but we were in so much of a fog that we'd have no idea what time it was. It was like we were never truly awake and never truly asleep.

We agreed early on, although I'm not sure if we ever verbally said it, that we had to disregard some of the passive-aggressive comments and snap reactions either of us would make when we were in extreme sleep deprivation. That's not really you. That's not really him. We'd brush it off quickly. Life's too short to make everything an argument.

You're getting through an ordeal in order to be present for your baby — and let's be clear, it's a really worthwhile one because that's the stuff that helps your baby feel super protected and cared for. You have to do the legwork. Then when your kid does adorable stuff you have no shame about posting the candid on every social media channel and blab about him to coworkers. You did the legwork. But nonetheless, it's an ordeal, and you would be wise to not take things personally. You wouldn't want him to do the same.

That covers those early weeks and months, sure, but what about when you are well into it? I think that's where the danger lies. I was well aware that the early going would be tough. Who says a newborn is going to be easy? Well, non-parents, probably. Dummies.

But I don't remember anyone ever talking much about the grind of it all after those first few weeks. It wasn't a long night here or there that had me start to turn into a person I didn't recognize. It was the months piling up where all the little sacrifices to make things work started to take their toll. And I wasn't taking care of myself as a result.

That's where *you* can come in, if that's sounding like a familiar scene.

My wife did a superb job at this. She knew something was off, but also didn't push too hard to make me snap out of it. Instead, she listened as I would confess that I was having a really difficult time. She would nod as I blurted out that I had some nights that I was pushed beyond the breaking point because babies and toddlers don't let up just because you've had a long day.

She soaked all that in. She did not try to fix it right away, or give me a big speech, or have me make promises I couldn't keep. And she then both gave me some leeway to figure things out while also increasing the amount of time I could just be sans kids. It went a long way, especially knowing there was accountability added since she would be more mindful to keep an eye out for it.

I think you're going to do a stellar job of being aware of how you are feeling personally and being vocal about needing a mental break; if you aren't, do it. After all, you're no good to your baby if you're a zombie. It's OK to ask someone to watch the baby for a few hours for the sole purpose of you just going to get a coffee or tea and reading a book by yourself.

Don't wait until you need a babysitter for an event or a

scheduling conflict. You need a break sometimes for nothing other than the break itself. Take up one of those offers to watch your kid; when someone says they'd love to help sometime, pin them down and make them pick a date that works for them, and if they balk, it wasn't a real offer.

In the same light, it is immensely helpful if you can keep an eye out on your partner's mental well-being (as he should for you, too). I'm telling you, if he hasn't done it before, he's not all of a sudden *now* going to be great about sticking his hand in the air and saying, "This isn't going well." But in this case, prod a little. Ask some questions. Take note if you see patterns.

I didn't speak up soon enough, but if I did, I am sure my wife would have made sure to find some extra times to give me some alone time, or talked through some strategies with me.

This is a reciprocal thing, by the way. When you support him, it makes it that much easier for him to do vice versa. Like sometimes, out of nowhere, I'll whisk the kids away for a few hours on a Saturday afternoon so my wife can do something in peace. It doesn't have to be a big deal, but it does have to actually happen — otherwise the dad is no better than your friend who would "love to watch that lil baby" but then never follows through.

Does a new dad need help? What to look for.

If you're looking out for little signs that he might need a step back or perhaps professional help, you can help him be a better dad for the long haul by checking in on him early and often. Some signs to keep an eye out for:

· He is increasingly vocal about not wanting to do things he used to be fine with

- He isn't smiling or laughing at things that otherwise would have cracked a smile
- He feels distant when you're in the car, like he can't focus
- He gets snippy about being asked to do things the first time you mention it
- He finds excuses to not do family events
- He gets almost over-excited at chances to do things with just the two of you
- He's more obsessed with being on his phone, but not for any particular purpose
- He's finding reasons to work on a "needed" project for hours on end, especially if it's in isolation, like fixing the car or doing yardwork
- He's over-the-top posting about the baby despite also constantly complaining about the same baby
- His hands seem tense all the time
- He's got a lot of mood swings going on, with no awareness of it

I don't mean any of this as if the onus is all on you to make sure everybody is fine. Wow, like you need even more things to worry about. I mean that out of the two of you, it's more likely you'll be in tune with what's really going on. I know I didn't pick up on my vibes until my wife would (nicely!) point out that yeah, I was being kind of a dick sometimes and it was because I was overwhelmed and not addressing it.

As a reminder, I am not a mental health expert, and seek professional guidance for anything you think warrants attention. This is just to help with conversations and spotting patterns!

But I can promise you that you're getting an authentic, honest reflection of parenting, and that is something I don't think happens often enough.

So when I tell you that there is more than a slim chance that your partner is going to go through a rough patch, I'm saying that from experience and from having honest conversations with other dads. I hope if and when you hit your own rough patch, you can lean on your partner and your friends.

My wife has several groups of friends who are moms, and they constantly support each other and have some real freaking honest discussions, which is impressive. Guys are more likely to be loners — even if they have lots of guy friends, do they have lots of guy friends who they talk about emotions with? Just because they are in a league together or always watch football together doesn't mean they ever really discuss deep topics. Doesn't mean it is any less of a friendship, it's just different. Fortunately for him, you are awesome and are there for him.

So if you see a few of the items in the list happening, I would strongly believe there's an underlying issue there that, at the least, would be worth a discussion. Is he feeling overwhelmed? I don't mean is he tired and wishes he could just watch an NFL game the whole way through without having to do something. I mean, is he starting to feel that on a daily basis he is doing an uphill battle just to get through, even if there are moments of happiness?

Does he feel like he's not in control enough of his life? For guys, that's a big one! We spent our whole life being told to be leaders who take control, and then a baby comes around who doesn't give a shit about that and runs the show now.

I found that finding things I can control helped. In particular I would keep busy when I was alone with the kids. When I was trying to just lounge around and unwind, I'd get so frustrated and on the verge of anger because kids do not care about what you're trying to do, and any crying or climbing all over me or spills would be that much more upsetting, like they were being rude when in fact they were just being toddlers.

By staying busy doing little chores around the house, I'd both be productive (woohoo!) and not mind if my kids were acting out, since I had something to focus on. They'd also be bored of me doing chores and would be more likely to play on their own. We'd still find time to eat together, to read and to bond, but I wasn't expecting something they couldn't give.

You can be even more amazing than you already are as a partner simply by saying it's OK and that you'd like to help. Your husband knowing he's not letting you down means more than you know.

Other steps parents can take to stay calm.

I can't say I've found some magic solution. I'm assuming the magic solution is being super wealthy and having nannies and butlers; rich people have problems, too, but they have the money to fix it. At least that's how it worked on *Fresh Prince*.

Still, most of what I've found that works has to do with mindset and self-care, which aren't exactly buzz words for dudes. Dads need to take the approach that self-care is not optional or somehow not "for guys."

Self-care is manly. Feeling better about yourself is manly. And, of course, self-care is extremely important for women, too.

Knowing that, I'm better about doing things if I have a tool (or an app!) to help. Up front, the biggest change was driven by using the Calm app, which helps you meditate and practice mindfulness every day. In fact, for months I made it a priority to use it every single morning before 6 a.m. so the kids weren't yet awake.

In case you saw the word "mindfulness" and freaked a little, mindfulness isn't a dogma thing. There's nobody you're praying to, so you can easily adapt it to whatever religion you practice or lack thereof. There's no chanting, no burning incense to Mother Nature and no $10,000 weekend retreats to find your zen (I am sure someone offers one, but you don't need it).

It's about being present. Truly present. Not stuck on what didn't go right before. Not worrying about what you have to do or what will happen. Just being in the moment. And when you have kids, we have an overabundance of both of those emotionally fraught areas, so being present sounds pretty sweet.

So for more than a year, I woke up every day before 6 a.m. It's my time. And it starts my day off on the right foot. (More recently, I've found pockets of time elsewhere in the day, but I still do get up earlier than I'd otherwise do.)

Depending on your job and your kids, this either seems late or insane. My kids generally can sleep through the night now (at least after they crawl in our bed), so I'm not dealing with the five-times-a-night wake-up like I used to; I'm not advising you to do likewise if you have a baby because dude, you need sleep. But instead of trying to squeeze every last moment of sleep and getting up around, say, 6:45 a.m., you can get a lot out of a little extra.

Here's what I get out of this as part of my routine:

- **Quiet.** On most days, I would get anywhere from 30-45

minutes before my daughter gets up (she's an early riser). That means absolute quiet; I'm not even turning on the lights. It's been there for the taking, and all this time I kept complaining that I never get enough of it. Sometimes you have to take what's given. Each morning, I'd sit in the same spot and turn on the Calm app. The app is super easy to use, and they have a lot of guided meditation (if you're like me and have no idea what to do, you want to go that route!). I did a 21 Days of Calm guide and by the end, you find yourself being more aware of how you feel, more alert of your trigger points, and more capable of finding that perfect spot of "now"—not worrying about what's to come, not regretting what's happened. If that doesn't describe what all parents need, I don't know what does.

- **The payoff of peace.** This makes it worth getting up, so I wouldn't need a ton of motivation. While you may think, "Wow, I would just fall right back to sleep if I try to meditate that early!" I found otherwise. It's more like that's an easy excuse for us to make so we don't have to put out some effort. Now, if your baby is up all night, sure! You gotta get some sleep. But if you have a decent sleep schedule, it's more a matter of prioritizing going to bed at a decent hour.
- **Starting the day on my terms.** The thing is, I had known for a long time what one of my toughest moments is each day. It's the morning rush. It's getting everyone dressed and fed and brushed, getting the house back in order, and dealing with all the inevitable "Where did that thing go we need?" plus trying to get myself ready. But what if, instead, I had a 30 minute head start? Even with 15 minutes for meditation, I could bang out some dishes, tidy up the den, maybe get a kid or two dressed as they meandered downstairs, and have

a bite to eat, all before I normally would be getting started. I used to think in my 20s that nothing is worth getting up early. This is.

- **Being awake before the kids are awake so I'm not starting off the day annoyed at *how* I woke up.** With babies, it can be impossible, given that most are waking up at all points in the night for no reason. But once you're in a routine, you start to be so protective of the sleep you get because you are now so aware of how valuable it is! So if I heard one of my kids come into the room crying because they're awake at 6 a.m., I'd get resentful and a little ticked since they woke me up. But if I'm already up? Problem solved. I'm greeting them with a smile, and both our days are better.

- **More time for my wife to sleep.** This is just a nice side effect. For the most part, she can keep sleeping a little longer, and that energy pays off mid-afternoon when I'm at work and she has all three kids by herself. There's not enough Starbucks in the world. My wife is one of the hardest working people I know, and she spends every day trying to be a super mom. If I can make her life easier, I need to do it.

Stay busy

Other than mindfulness, I also suggest dads in particular think about what is happening when they are getting frustrated. If they are like me, it might be because they wish they were able to "do something productive" and they can't because they are taking care of the baby. Except taking care of the baby *is* being productive!

Still, if I'm with the kids all night by myself, I do so much better mentally if I don't just lay down and unwind. That seems counterintuitive, but stay with me. What I realized, at least for me, is that the act of trying to unwind after work only has benefits for me if I can actually unwind. My kids, who haven't seen me all day, want to play and bounce around and read and show me things. This is not unwinding! This involves a lot of energy. Sure, I could do that for a few minutes and let them cuddle up with me and we can watch a movie, do dinner and call it a night (and some days, that's all I can do ... like I said, this isn't magic, and parenting isn't Instagram).

But what happened a lot was that I'd sit down and instantly feel like I didn't want to move for awhile, and of course, that's not what my toddlers had in mind so I'd get frustrated and a little ticked (Do you see a pattern?) that they weren't down for my plan, and nobody would really get what they wanted.

Or I'd get a sense of their mood —if they wanted to be cuddled a lot and I was trying to do a million things, maybe I was the one who needed to slow down, because my frustration wasn't based on realistic expectations.

Instead, here's what I am doing much more often:

Picturing them happy: Before I enter the house after work, I do a trick my therapist taught me. I picture everyone smiling. That puts a smile on my face, and even if it's hectic in there, I've got a better attitude to deal with it.

Doing something with them right away: Before my brain has the chance to tell me to unwind after a long day at work, I try to do something active with the kids. Maybe it's just playing around. Maybe it's a walk. Maybe it's doing a puzzle. But it ensures that I'm starting off positive, for them and for me, and that's already going to help stave off those frustrated feelings. After all, it's not their fault!

Get chores done all night long. If you're like me, mounting frustrations can lead to you losing energy. (You know how some days, you just feel drained all day? That's probably more a stress thing than a sleep thing.) If you lose energy, one of the first things to go is your will to do chores around the house. But all that does is just create compounding problems—those chores don't go away, and now you're mad about having a shit-ton of things to do.

Instead, often after doing something with my kids on a weeknight, I'd completely clean up from dinner so my wife wasn't coming home to a bunch of dishes (we all know the visual isn't exactly welcoming, so that would suck for her to come home and see dinner wasn't cleaned up yet). Or instead of relaxing while my kids played (God, it's so much easier when they can start entertaining themselves, but if you're not there yet and can strap your kid on you, it's the same idea), I'd vacuum or do the laundry or weed wack. And by staying busy, I wasn't allowing myself the opportunity to get mad and frustrated; I was being productive, and being productive for me is something I really value. I'm channeling my energy. (At least when I remembered to be on top of it.)

Even with all the mindfulness or great approaches in the world, you're still going to lose it sometimes. But I am making sure, more and more, to pause before I react and even step out of the room if needed. It's OK to say the moment is overwhelming, step out, count to 10 and go back in. They aren't going to remember. (Calm even has a Take 90, which is a 90-second meditation solely intended to help you calm the f*&@ down. It's magical.)

I don't know where your partner is on the "Need to Chill Out" index as a new parent. But I think a lot more parents than we know are dealing with a metric ton of frustration, anger, doubt, worry and so many other day-ruining feelings. Parenting is a lot! Babies and toddlers do not make sense, and they won't make sense tomorrow either. They aren't going to take it easy on you because you're at the end of your rope. They may, in fact, grab that rope and light it on fire and then shit completely up their backs just for the thrill. My daughter has pooped in her underwear while laughing in my face! It's psychotic!

But you both can find some peace with how you react to it all. And maybe laugh a little, too.

Because sometimes you have to laugh through the tears.

11

What to expect when you're expecting expectations.

You both need to remember you're just two humans trying to do your best.

Things that have changed about me since I became a father:

1. I am more in touch with my feelings and more aware of what others are going through
2. I have more purpose than ever before and my convictions are deeper because the impact is greater
3. I have no idea why I ever felt broke before having kids
4. I give less of a shit about dumb stuff because I don't have time to give it any thought
5. I age in dog years now

Becoming a parent is like dropping food coloring into water. You can't separate the two once you do it. It's forever changed.

I think. I'm not awesome with chemistry.

Parenting is like a before/after makeover on a talk show. Except instead of a glamorous new look, you emerge as a fundamentally new person. And your new look is more "I can wear this three days in a row, right?"

We all get that things are totally different, and often in incredible, awesome ways. You can't buy feelings like you get as a proud new parent. You can't even really explain it (Although shows like *Parenthood* did a pretty good job of it!). But it seems that trying to get a sense of how men are transforming is the most vexing. Why do some guys emerge like Clark Kent from a phone booth, and others remain robotic, functioning exactly the same even when life demands more?

How do guys change as they go from bro to dad?

I hear from moms who wish upon wish her husband or boyfriend would "see the light" and grow up and take some responsibility. That, by the sheer force of having a baby around, he'll stop playing Xbox all the time and maybe get serious about having a job, not staying out to 1 a.m. every night and treating you with respect. That a guy that has shown zero sense of responsibility will suddenly become Mr. Dad. He's not going to. That's not how it works.

And women become kick-ass moms anyway, despite the absentee dads.

Fortunately, a lot of guys aren't in that category. They just need a little nudge, a little focus, a little urgency to become parents anyone would be proud to have.

He seems to have his head on straight, right? He does romantic gestures. He listens. You always imagine he'll be an amazing father.

And then you have a baby.

What's a realistic scenario for what he'll be like as a father:

A) He finds a way to keep everything going. He's exactly the same guy you married and more. You're finding new ways to appreciate him as he seems to pull off superhuman feats. You kinda love bragging about him to other moms, those snarky bitches.

B) He crumbles after three straight weeks of no sleep. He snaps at you for no reason. He grumbles about chores he used to do without even being asked. He spends the whole night when he gets home on the phone, browsing aimlessly, rather than talking to you. He's a shell of the guy he was before.

I think you already know the answer is A and B. That some days he'll be Phil from *Modern Family*, keeping a sense of humor and doing anything for his family and not letting up on the romance. And other times, maybe for an hour, maybe for a month, he can be a jerk.

I can't say this enough, but unless you've had some honest conversations with other new parents, it's unlikely you are getting a good feel for how your partner is going to be based on Instagram pics of your friend's husband cradling their newborn. Because that doesn't show you if they squabbled right before they walked to the beach. Or how he's feeling inside. Or if this is the first time all day he helped out.

I've been both sides, for sure.

Becoming a dad made me realize I was capable of things I never would have dreamed of before. It makes you love so much harder. I love my kids real hard. It makes me teary-eyed sometimes just thinking about what I would do for them. It makes you appreciate the little things that you took for granted, like the sound of laughter, the feel of little fingers holding your hand ... or sleeping three hours in a row (I never knew that was a commodity).

It forces you to prioritize and stop worrying about dumb stuff. I often tell my coworkers that nothing in my full-time job will ever be as complicated as being a dad, so I try not to stress out too much.

Sometimes I feel like a wonderful father, at least based on feedback from some very tough and tiny customers. Some days, I almost relish the challenge of taking all three kids to a grocery store just to see if I could freaking do it, especially when they were babies. And as I'd track down the only available shopping cart with the kiddy car on the front and the kids would laugh through the aisles and everyone would go home smiling, you can't help but think, "Alright, not too shabby dude."

What to realistically expect from new dads.

Every day your partner needs to soak in those moments. You should soak in your own, too. It can't be all beating yourself up all the time. You are doing an incredible thing every day. Don't let the mommy Facebook groups and Internet comment sections get you down. Nobody knows what they are doing.

Got it?

Unfortunately, if a mom only imagined the "perfect dad" scenario, then she will be so frustrated when option B inevitably happens at some point.

Give yourself time to think of what you can realistically expect from him — and yourself! — and in those moments of frustration, remember that it's impossible for anyone to be everything all the time. He's going to have tough days. So are you. You can't be too hard on yourself.

He's going to have a day when the baby crying drives him up the wall. You'll have a stretch when you just can't do one more diaper blowout. And it won't seem reasonable, and you'll feel bad afterward for snapping, but when you have realistic expectations that you don't have to be perfect, then you're giving each other permission to be real.

If the tough days seem like they are mounting, let him know. Be honest. This isn't about criticism. This is about being fair to both of you. You need an engaged, energetic partner so that *you* don't have to be that person all the time. And you also want him to feel supported.

You're in this together. That's the awesome thing. And both of you being realistic, being honest and being up front about the tidal wave of emotions you're going through can only help.

Because when the baby has cried for like 251,151 hours in a row, ain't nobody acting sane anymore.

That's what to expect what you're expecting. Expect that you'll be parents of the year some days and the very next minute find yourself muttering under your breath.

You're in it together. That's the beauty of it.

12

Dad turn: You are going to be a great dad.

Once a new dad realizes he doesn't have to be perfect, he can maximize his fatherhood potential.

Hand this book over to your left or to your right. Whatever side he sleeps on. It's time for a pep talk to that amazing guy you are raising a child with (And then make sure you read this, too!).

Hey man.

So your wife/girlfriend/it's complicated person just told you to read this chapter. You're looking at a book called *The New Mom's Guide to New Dads* and wondering, "WTF?"

Is this guy trying to speak for me? He doesn't even know me!

Why should I listen to him?

Here's the deal: I've been in your shoes. I've been a brand-new dad — at one point, three kids three and under — who was looking everywhere for some answers, for some reassurance, for some other dads to give him some guidance and a slap on the back.

Because this stuff just doesn't come as naturally to us.

Like me, you've had that "What do you even DO with a baby?" thought cross your mind, maybe ever since the pee stick was waved in front of you like an insanely accurate magic 8 ball. ("Your future is tired.")

You've never been a dad before. Or perhaps never even held a baby before. And you can feel the anxiety and the uncertainty rising within you.

- What if I hurt the baby?
- Why do people expect I'll know what I'm doing?
- I've never even changed a diaper! Do I crate train them? Wait, that doesn't sound right.
- What if I mess up and my wife gets mad?
- What if I mess up and I can't fix it?
- What am I expected to do? I don't know how to swaddle jack squat.
- What if I'm left alone with the baby and I don't know what to do and the baby is crying and there's poop everywhere and I don't know how to use the bottles and I can't remember any nursery rhymes and what temperature are you even supposed to make the bath and oh god oh god oh god.

That sort thing.

Sound familiar?

You feel helpless, because it seems every other dad out there has their shit together, and you're standing there in the middle of Target, staring at eight different car seats that all look the freaking same and yet you're supposed to pick out the safest one. (*Hint: If it's on the market, it's passed all the federal safety guidelines. Find one with easy release anchor tethers and the most adjustability, and you're set.)*

You hear how excited your wife is about the baby, and how she just knows what to do, whether it's with the pregnancy or with your newborn already here.

You're not an idiot. You know you should be involved. That's not the problem. If it was, you wouldn't be reading this.

The problem is "I want to help with the baby, but I don't know how!" Right? Or maybe it's more "I think I'm doing a decent job, but it'd be cool to know for sure."

How do you go from one second being just some guy to the next being a father people expect should have answers?

It seems like nobody tells you, or at least they won't give you any straight answers. You get talked to like you're a clueless sitcom dad. A laundry list of dad advice-style blog posts and books exist, and many are assuming you are just a beer-guzzling, sports-loving, me-Tarzan you-Jane simpleton. (OK for me it's mostly hard cider because I couldn't tell a lager from an IPA if you paid me. Don't judge.)

Here's what you see a lot of when it comes to puzzling new dad advice. **These are direct quotes from the popular Baby Bump App that your partner probably installed on her phone:**

Lately it may seem like your partner's girlfriends and mother know more about what's going on with the baby than you do. If this is the case, it's time for you to get in the game and make your voice heard. Let the mommy-to-be know that you're interested in everything she has to say and all that's going on with the baby. Ask her questions about how she feels and what sort of things the baby has done each day ... she'll realize you've felt left out and that you really want to be involved.

That's a sad, tired take, man.

The premise is that at some point during the pregnancy, you, an idiot, suddenly realize, "Hey, maybe I should see what that whole baby thing is my wife keeps yammering on and on about." As if men aren't capable of being attentive or caring about the baby without an app saying "You know what would be a good idea? Talking about the baby."

You've been hearing a lot about the process of labor from your buddies, who seem to take great pleasure in emphasizing the messy, gross parts ... **remember that even though it may not look pleasant, the end result is worth it!**

WTF. Now we're assuming you can't handle being included in childbirth because you might see a placenta, because it's the 1950s and oooooh icky girl parts. And also, I can't remember any of my "buddies" having a conversation about placentas.

Although you still have a few weeks until the baby arrives ... it's never too early to start thinking about baby-proofing your house. Put child safety locks on all openable compartments, from cabinets and drawers to the refrigerator and toilet. And don't forget about those door handles — apply childproof grips that prevent the handle from turning.

That's some crazy nonsense right there. If you are putting childproof locks on the toilet a YEAR before your kid has even a prayer of opening a toilet lid, you're making life tougher on yourself, and that also seems like a solution in search of a problem. Should you take charge of childproofing? Sure, that makes sense. But you put childproof locks on the cabinets before the baby is even born, and you're asking for it. In fact, if they can't even turn on their stomach yet, you will stress everyone out.

Just as you'd schedule an appointment at work, plan to set aside time to spend with your baby girl. Even 10 minutes here and there can provide with valuable bonding opportunities."

Oh you've got to be kidding. This isn't a Google Calendar setting: "9 a.m. Hold Baby, Smile, Set Down." Now we're setting the fatherhood bar at "Set 10 minutes aside to be a decent human being." Your baby isn't a goal to set, like hitting the gym twice a week.

When the excited expression lights up on your wife's face, don't just sit there: Ask her to place your hand where the baby is moving.

So glad you cleared that up! Don't sit there like an ape. Maybe interact with your wife. Got it.

"Showing up" is a really low bar for being a dad. Do better.

If that's all you're looking to do, well, you did it. You're, um, a good father now. You might even get commended by strangers for doing basic stuff like pushing the baby stroller or being out on your own with the baby.

But you want more than that.

You want to make your partner feel supported, to make your kid feel loved and to make yourself feel included in parenting in a deep, transformative way.

I want that for you, man!

I want that for you because being a dad who is heavily involved is the best feeling you ever will have. That's why I put together this book for both of you! That and I needed to keep busy with a big-boy activity that did not involve talking cartoon animals or applesauce pouches.

You're already doing a great thing by spending time in reading how to be a kick-ass dad — so many guys don't put forth any effort. You know it and I know it. And not in a judge-y, looking down your nose at them kind of way. But in a disappointed we-can't-all-rise-to-the-occasion way. **Society already doesn't**

expect as much from fathers. We have to do better.

I'm here to say you are so going to nail this.

I'm also here to say that I have felt completely, utterly helpless before. I get it.

(Heads up: I've got a breastfeeding story coming. Please get used to breastfeeding stories. Whether your partner nurses or not, you're going to hear sooooo many breastfeeding stories. If you learn nothing else, learn that breastfeeding is very difficult for many moms, it's not as naturally easy as you'd think it is, and that their frustration from that may be among their biggest as new moms.)

How I felt helpless as a dad ... and learned how to help.

My son, Elliott, was born a month ahead of schedule. The night before Mother's Day, I was up late applying wall decals and finishing touches to his ocean-themed nursery.

My wife, Sara, was going to help, but she was just not feeling it. She went to bed early, and I kept plowing through, wrapping up the finishing touches later that night.

I go to bed around 11 p.m. An hour later, Sara taps me on the shoulder and lets me know she thinks she's having contractions eight minutes apart. As if that's something you tap someone on the shoulder about.

You tap someone on the shoulder to say, "Hey, did you leave the light on downstairs?" You don't tap if you want to say, "I think a baby may be exiting my vagina rather quickly."

I can see her, calmly sitting with an iPhone app, timing things out. She's not sure yet if it's a false alarm. I, on the other hand, freak out.

I start throwing things in a bag. We had planned to put together an overnight bag that very Sunday, figuring a month ahead ought to do it. Nope.

"I'm not going to be the a-hole husband who sits around while his wife is going into labor!" I exclaimed to anyone and no one, frantically throwing things in a bag.

Fortunately, my zen-like wife made me realize that even if this was the real deal, we were far from having to go to the hospital. (You may hear in a birth class about waiting until contractions are about five minutes apart, lasting a minute long each, as a good indicator it's time to go. If a baby head pops out ... you waited too long.)

We stayed up all night watching *Mad Men* and the *Cosby Show*. In hindsight, bad choice. Thanks, Bill Cosby.

Around 7 a.m., we went to the hospital. Just before pulling away from the house, I looked at Sara and said, "Let's pause for a moment just in case this is the last time it's ever just the two of us."

It was.

Our son was born at six pounds, five ounces — not bad considering he had a month to go!

Officially, that timeline meant he was "late preterm." Not an official premie (he avoided the NICU), but not quite ready for showtime.

Why was this important?

Breastfeeding.

If you ever want a reminder that your girlfriend/wife is a miracle worker, watch her breastfeed. It doesn't even make SENSE.

There is milk coming out of her body! Food! Just, right there! Where you used to hang out!

The thing is, although we were extremely into the idea of breastfeeding our son, late preterms don't have the mouth size and skills yet to be great at latching.

And that's when, just days into fatherhood, I had my first serious case of "I want to help with the baby, but I don't know hows". I think that's what WebMD calls it.

The good news is that our hospital had incredibly helpful lactation consultants. (Insurance covers this, by the way, in many cases.)

The bad news is that doesn't mean our son magically became great at latching on.

His weight was dropping, partially because he wasn't getting enough through breastfeeding. He was down under six pounds, and he was jaundiced.

We had done everything we were supposed to do ahead of time. We went to a breastfeeding class. We read up on the subject, and had the Boppy pillow.

But parenting is a series of realities that harshly, rudely knock down expectations.

Elliott didn't care if we had talked to experts. He just wanted food.

Not long after we had left the hospital, we had an appointment to see the lactation consultant.

We were exhausted. We were bewildered. We were so happy to have Elliott, and yet so baffled about what he needed and wanted.

Why didn't this just work?

The way the appointments are set up, Elliott was weighed at the start, then my wife would nurse him until he was done, and then he would get weighed again to see the difference in weight, like a wrestler trying to make a weight class.

When you're a late preterm, weight is basically everything.

Yes, they could tell when it's a matter of ounces. I hope to

God it's not like that after I eat Chipotle burritos.

Elliott, with a tinge of yellow on his skin from a touch of jaundice, was the most beautiful thing I had ever seen at that point, and all I wanted to do was take care of him like my dad took care of me or like all the dads in the TGIF lineup took care of their sitcom kids, at least.

And yet here we were, sitting in a tiny office, with a consultant looking at a scale and then telling us that our son wasn't gaining enough weight.

Sara started to tear up. I felt tears in my eyes looking at my wife, who I loved so much for so many different reasons, feeling helpless, like she wasn't going to be a good mom because she "couldn't do the thing moms are designed to do," as she and others often put it. Of course she was going to be a great mom, but that doesn't mean she felt like it.

But here's the thing.

Parenting, you find out quickly, isn't about having all the right answers. It's about adapting. You are going to be so good at adapting after becoming a parent. Nothing will really phase you anymore.

We got a plan from the lactation consultant. A plan that, looking back, I can't believe we actually pulled off. A plan that I can now say not only helped me get super involved right away, but also gave me confidence that yeah, sure, I can do this dad thing.

Here was our new feeding schedule:

Sara would nurse Elliott as long as she could. This would take anywhere from 10-20 minutes. And he wouldn't get much.

When she was done, she'd continue pumping as much as she could.

Meanwhile, I would take a plastic syringe and fill it with an ounce of breast milk. I'd attach a thin plastic tube to one end, and tape the other end to my index finger. Then, holding Elliott, I'd slowly feed him by putting the tubed finger in his mouth — giving him something to suck on — while pressing down on the syringe. We're talking ultra slow on this. I'd take 20 minutes to get him to take maybe half an ounce. It was hard for him to keep awake, and some days he wouldn't really take anything and we'd feel like crying again because we just wanted him to grow and be healthy. On a side note, this kid eats two cups of yogurt, two bananas, a quesadilla, rice and beans, and dessert in one sitting like it's nothing now. I am glad I don't need to push beans through a tube.

One of us would clean up the pumping supplies and the syringe to be ready for the next feeding, while the other would change him.

Did you add up the time? About 15 minutes for the first part, plus about 20 minutes for the second, and another 10 for cleaning equals 45 minutes. We were supposed to feed him upward of 12 times a day. So about 45 minutes out of every two hours was taken up with nothing but the feeding process.

The other hour was taken up trying to get him to sleep — he slept in 15-20 minute chunks in the early weeks — or trying to eat something ourselves or maybe get something else done as our very helpful in-laws were on hand to keep up with housework so we didn't end up on "Hoarders."

When you add all that up, there was quite literally no time to do anything. I remember being so tired I couldn't speak complete sentences.

"Man, Andy," you're thinking. "This doesn't sound like a pep talk."

How you can get new dad confidence faster.

This was a temporary stage in Elliott's life. He soon got big enough to be great at breastfeeding and started gaining a pound a week. He went from the bottom 25th percentile for height and weight to the 97th percentile for both. Now, as a grade schooler, he's usually the tallest kid when he's playing with friends.

I went from having no confidence that I could do this to thinking, "If I can do that, I can handle anything."

I want to help you get to that Point B faster and easier.

I had really, really limited experience with babies before Elliott came around. Let's just say that feeding a baby breast milk with a tube wasn't on my list of skills.

I had a Cabbage Patch doll once. Does that count?

That's the thing. It's incredible how fast you will pick things up.

You won't believe how adept you'll get at:

- Changing a diaper in a parking lot. Or the floor of a mechanic's bathroom.
- Vacuuming and holding a baby at the same time. (Baby carriers are lifesavers.)
- Cleaning up throw up on you and the baby and changing her entire outfit in time for you to still get out the door for work.
- Eating dinner with one hand.
- Actually, doing pretty much everything with one hand. Or no hands. You're going to get prison strong with one arm.

So why is that?

Why do guys feel so ill-prepared to be dads when, given the

chance, we can be all-stars?

Because guys don't grow up hearing about how they'll be great dads one day. They don't pretend to play house as a dad. Nobody holding a baby assumes the teenage boy probably should get a turn.

Some of that is old sexist stuff, the same way you don't hear a lot of people telling young girls how they can become CEOs.

Some of that is genetic stuff — there really is some maternal instincts that guys, of course, don't get born with the way women do.

But regardless, you don't really think about becoming a dad — let alone a good father — until an "Oops! Pregnant!" moment and you start realizing what the hell that means.

Your wife has likely been spending some of her life thinking about becoming a mom or what it would be like to be a mom. It doesn't guarantee a woman is going to be an awesome mother right away or have a clue what she's doing, but it means she'll probably have a better shot at a fast start.

You probably spent ... well, let's see. How long ago did you find out your wife was pregnant? That amount of time.

There's catching up to do.

The first thing you can do is realize that if you put in the effort to help with the baby, soothe the baby and nurture the baby, you are going to be such an amazing father.

It's guaranteed.

Here's how I can guarantee you're going to be a great dad:

- Would you do whatever you could to protect your wife (or partner)?
- Would you hold her hair and rub her back if she's throwing

up?

- Would you take care of the dishes and clean up beyond what you normally do because she's too busy and you know she'd appreciate it?
- Would you get over it if she snaps at you for no reason because she's exhausted or sick?
- Would you put her needs above your own?

That's love, right? That's what being in love is all about — doing things you would never do for just anyone because that person means the world to you.

Substitute "wife/partner" for "baby."

You are going to love your kid so freaking much. It's going to be the thing that gets you through long nights and long days.

You would do absolutely anything to protect your baby — and that's what a good father does, too.

You would clean off your baby and rub his back when he's spitting up — and that's what a good father does, too.

You would take care of the dishes and clean up beyond what you normally do because your partner needs time for breastfeeding or bottlefeeding — and that's what a good father does, too.

You would get over it when your baby screams at you for no reason because she's likely exhausted or sick — and that's what a good father does, too.

You would put your baby's needs above your own — and that's what a good father does, too.

I'm not even saying you will automatically, instantaneously, be in love with your baby. I know some dads, it's before the baby is born. Others, it's the moment the baby arrives. And for others, they love their son or daughter right away, but that real, deep, passionate, "I'll do anything for them" emotion might not come until a little bit after they spend some time with the baby. They don't get the benefit of having the baby inside them for nine months to get a head start.

But it'll happen.

Before you worry about anything else, know that the love you will have for your baby will help you overcome so much of your fear and anxiety.

You'll just GO FOR IT because you truly want to help any way you can.

You'll still make mistakes.

You'll still be banging your heads sometimes because you're exhausted or don't know why the baby is mad or feel frustrated.

But you'll have such a true and honest love for your kid, man ... I can't wait for you to experience it. If there's a magic elixir of any kind when it comes to fatherhood, that's it.

Think through why you're apprehensive about fatherhood.

You don't feel unsure you'll be able to take care of your wife for the rest of your life, do you?

You love her a ton. You know you'll figure it out as you go.

Your son or daughter will bring that same sense of confidence once you make that connection.

What if you're not "into the baby" yet?

At one point, I heard from a pregnant mom who was worried why her boyfriend wasn't "into" their baby. He just wanted to work on his car. Does he really love his car more than his unborn child, she asked?

My honest assessment:

The guy is probably being a bit of an insensitive jerk, but

there's also a reason he's connecting with a car and not a baby.

The car, I told her, has long been a physical thing he can touch, experience and cherish.

The baby? Up to that point, the baby was a series of ultra-sounds, conversations and possibilities. The baby hasn't been "real." Tangible. Holdable.

You can't cuddle with an ultrasound. Don't try. Creepy.

The mom was feeling baby kicks and had that whole lifetime-geared-toward-motherhood thing I just talked about. She was in the baby mindset, and he was catching up.

Does that mean you should be more attentive, ask more questions and try to be more involved if you know that sounds like you? Hell yes. At the least, that's what you do as a supportive partner. Maybe you understand cars or sports or politics or fitness or 15th century art a lot better than you understand babies. That's fine, but the onus is on you to catch up, because you don't get a free pass. It's not like she gets to opt out.

It's easy to get into something you already understand, and even easier to put off becoming passionate about something you know little about that someone keeps telling you to become passionate about.

I love baseball. I don't understand soccer. Even if my city was getting a new soccer team and my wife was getting me lifelong season passes, it'd be hard for me to get pumped about it until I went to games for awhile. I'd stay focused on baseball, because at least I know and love it.

And that's just a sport. Make that your own flesh and blood — where getting involved means you also have responsibilities and can mess things up — and it makes sense why some guys don't seem to connect with an unborn baby or a fresh newborn.

If you're saying, "That's her thing. That's a mom thing. That's a grandmother thing." or "I can just financially support the baby. I can just stay out of the way. The baby can get all it needs from my wife." ... Man, c'mon.

There is no amount of fatherhood advice that will overcome you not letting your guard down and opening yourself up to being a dad.

You and I both know the best scenario for your baby is for you to go all in.

Don't let yourself get in the way. Everything else is an excuse.

You can do this.

13

Fatherhood redefines manliness.

Fatherhood means guys stop needing to prove how manly they are — or at least it should.

I have never, ever been a manly man.

To be very clear, I have always been quite aware of this. Growing up I didn't do "guy stuff" well; I never rode ATVs, didn't hunt, didn't watch pro wrestling, and I was a skinny, glasses-wearing nerd before being a nerd was cool.

As an adult, I never liked beer, never got into MMA, have never known much about cars, never got a man cave or wanted one and generally always had more female friends than male friends because most of the time I'd have a difficult time bonding with guys.

My brother would be a much better example of a "manly man." When something breaks in my house, he's the first person I call. Without ever receiving formal training, I've seen him completely take apart our dryer that had stopped tumbling, fix it and put it back together. I know how to *use* the dryer. These are not equal skills.

He can fix most anything, drive a stick shift, change his car oil and have lengthy conversations about tractors and agriculture. He has big, strong hands and a permanent tan from working outside all the time.

I'm on the other end of the spectrum to the point you might be surprised we're related. I spent college days doing musicals. I enjoy clothes shopping. I will openly watch Lifetime Christmas movies (and play a fun game with my wife of guessing the entire plot just from the movie description). I can do some basic car maintenance — learning how to replace air filters has saved me a ton of money — and am not a complete idiot with tools, but no one will call me a "handyman." I love watching and talking about sports, but more about the behind-the-scenes transactions and the stats. I have a beard, which took me 49 years to grow. I have dainty writer's fingers and being in the sun too long makes me burst into flames like a pasty supernova.

My brother is absolutely a manly man. He also happens to be a pretty great dad and person.

What's the definition of manliness?

What I've learned since becoming a dad is that I can be a different kind of manly man, too. What is considered manly changes when you're wearing a baby.

It seems that now I can feel manly as a dad and still be the guy who is very aware of Meredith Grey's latest drama while wearing a bow tie and drinking Malibu Bay Breezes.

Being a manly man, hell, even just being a man in 2020, doesn't have to mean what we all grew up thinking it meant. It's not just *Mad Men*-types, all brooding and throwing back

Scotch and acting aloof. It's not just *Duck Dynasty*-types, all camo and guns and thick beards.

You can be a manly man and have tattoos and drink whiskey and love *Die Hard*. You can be a manly man and do none of those things. Because as it turns out, it's not a series of activities and body types and hobbies that defines your manliness.

Your partner is going to spend fatherhood figuring out what it means for him to be a man. Here's the secret:

It's how you act that makes you a man.

Has he been trying to figure out what manliness is while he's been up to his ears in diapers and bottles? Being a dad can add to the confusion.

He's been told for years that manly men types shouldn't be expected to do much as dads because, you know, they gotta bring home the bacon or something. Because a man hunts and a woman rears the kids (such a weird phrase). Because a man provides and a woman nurtures, with no gray area in between.

And then you factor in how men are viewed as parents — with a very low bar to hurdle. So men end up getting unfettered praise for doing basic things like changing diapers and watching the kids ("Oh, is dad babysitting tonight?" — things strangers say in the store for no reason).

All of that gives mixed signals to guys. It makes it seem like being an involved parent is, on some level, not what a "manly man" does because that means choosing your kid over going out to a sports bar, or sometimes choosing your family over your career progress, or spending weekends taking your kid to birthday parties rather than spending time playing *Call of Duty*. As if it's an either/or proposition. Or that being a dad can't suffice.

What makes me feel manly.

I'm only representing one dad. But for whatever it's worth, I can tell you that I never feel as manly as when I've had my toddlers crawling all over me, or when I've got all three in our "walking train" holding hands as we go through a parking lot, or when I have them run toward me to give me a hug.

I could work on an oil rig. I could play for the Steelers. I could shave with a hunting knife while fighting Chuck Norris with a boa constrictor I caught with my bare hands. And that would still not make me feel as manly. Those are *activities you do.* **Being a father is *who you are.***

He doesn't have to be a dad to be manly. Any guy can treat others with respect, look out for those less fortunate and leave the world better than when they entered it. A glance at the news on any day shows you how badly we need men to behave better. I don't even feel like women are demanding perfection! They are asking for us to behave the same way they are expected to act.

And by the way, guys shouldn't be praised for not being a d-bag around women, the same way they don't deserve it for simply caring for their kids. Nobody needs a trophy because of some #notallmen B.S., like we should honor him for not grabbing a colleague's butt. Likewise, nobody needs a medal because he showed up for parent-teacher conferences; I hope that is not the takeaway he has from involved parenthood. Neither makes him a "real man." It just makes him a decent human being.

Being a dad is built-in manliness if you're willing to embrace it, far more than he could achieve by doing all the stereotypical stuff. I think it's awesome and impressive that you can install your own brakes or wire your own home theatre or can start a fire with nothing but a rubber band and a paperclip. Those don't build a legacy, though.

Small steps of involved parenthood create larger paths of long-term impact.

He can try any of these, but the goal is to have him equate "I'm doing something with my kid" and "I am killing it as a guy today." How do you do that? Well, *you* won't be able to, as that's going to need to be his own journey. But it helps if he feels empowered to have lots of opportunities, and if he feels regularly supported; knowing that you love how he's trying to take this kind of thing on will mean a lot, even if he doesn't say it.

He can do this by:

- **Taking the baby out on his own to do something that he usually would rely on you for.** Do you usually get the groceries or do the doctor visits? Tag, he's it.
- **Being in charge of bedtime.** Maybe you do the nursing/feeding, but he changes your son and rocks him to sleep after reading him a story. I spent so many hours rocking my kids to sleep (and having my arms fall asleep #twinsdad). Men like having ownership of things. Great! Now he's got a thing.
- **Orrrrr getting your kid ready in the morning.** Depending on schedules, maybe getting up with the baby first thing, changing the diaper and putting on the outfit for the day is his thing, on top of getting the diaper bag ready and so forth. When he starts telling other guys how he's handling this, you know you're onto something. Especially if he "invents" ways to improve the morning routine and brags about it to

others. (As long as his invention doesn't drive you insane. Otherwise, I'd say let him do his thing because that's his way of showing enthusiasm and ownership. If it's causing more harm than good, reroute that enthusiasm.)

- **Finding a routine thing that he can take the baby to all the time.** Maybe he's got a guy's night that's just for the guys, but there's another time when it wouldn't be a big deal if he had the baby with him; I'm going to take a guess that people expect you to have your baby with you all the time, even if you're with friends, so he should be expected to sometimes juggle the same way. Being manly can mean that he's capable of doing both — and it gives him ample time to show off his daughter!

None of this means he stops being who he is. He doesn't need to entirely change his personality!

I think of it as enhancing what it means to be a man. For him, it is acceptable and commendable and imperative that he never loses sight of how powerful being an involved father can be.

Being a dad is confusing. Being a man shouldn't be.

14

How dads (and moms!) can take more solo time.

It needs to be a two-way street. He takes more responsibility while you take a step back (even if you're holding your breath!).

Months in advance, I knew it would come to this.

Me. Hannah. Quinn. Daddy, daughter and daughter. A guy and a couple of two-year-olds. Just the three of us for a long weekend, with no mommy in sight.

If you're a new dad, that might run a chill down your spine. I've heard from lots of fathers who recoil like a cobra at the thought of spending one-on-one time with their baby. Not because they don't love their kid. It's because they don't freaking understand their baby, and are pretty sure that they'll get arrested for child neglect or something because surely the cops will know this poor sap is screwing up his son long term.

I just got through my long weekend — a set-up that came because my wife took our three-year-old son to California to see family — unscathed. I'd go so far as to say it went well.

That's not an accident.

Now, sure, I've had to do it many times at this point, either for a day or overnight. But this was the longest stretch my wife had been away from the girls. I had already served up karma by leaving her the weekend before to go speak at a conference. But you and I both know nobody bats an eye at a mom being left alone with the kids. Ridiculous, but true.

It's still a bit unusual to see a dad out with his kids by himself.

I'm hoping you can be part of a movement to start to change that, but that will take time.

Why some dads are scared to go out with their baby.

At this point, it's second nature for me to take the kids out by myself. Some of you moms have told me that your husband never takes the baby out. I'm going to take an educated guess here and say that has nothing to do with ability. It has a lot to do with being afraid of failing. Guys really, really hate looking bad at doing things and not knowing what we're doing.

Nothing encapsulates that more than a dad out alone with a baby, as babies are insane and will sometimes smile while they throw up on you. Toddlers will cry and laugh at the same time, which is psychotic. So while many moms will just think "Whatever, I'll make this work, I'm not staying in the house!" some dads think "Um, rather not."

I'm telling your partner to embrace the challenge. He can send you out for the morning for "me" time and play with your baby and feed them breakfast. Have errands to do? He can take your toddler to a buffet (quick food!) while you get to go into stores a thousand times faster. I'm sure you secretly wouldn't mind errands as much if you could get them done quickly (or not at all — it's your time!). He gets to eat and spend time with your kid, and you get some alone time. Wins for everyone.

Because dude, he can handle a meal. Or a morning. Or getting the baby down for a nap and sending you out to get a manicure. Every time he does that, he becomes more confident as a dad and also making it easier for you to get some alone time as well. Make sense?

"Sure, Andy," you may be thinking, "He can handle two hours, but you are talking about three-plus days alone! How the hell does he do that? What happens if he can't get our kid to stop crying? What if he forgets the diaper bag? WHAT HAPPENS IF A TERRORIST ATTACKS OUR HOUSE?"

He can take a breath, and so can you (maybe it's just him freaking out!). He can do this. If he stinks at it, I've been told Kate Spade sunglasses also make moms feel better.

The no-fail steps to a successful weekend of solo parenting, dad edition (pass this along!).

Stick to a schedule: With mom not around, you don't want any more change than is needed. If there's a strict nap time (and my God, please do strict nap times. Biggest mistake we made with our first kid!), stick to it. Bath every night? Better do that, too. It'll be tempting if your daughter is in a great mood to blow through lunch time or skip the bath if they are super mad, but you'll pay for it.

Get support: I had work obligations during that weekend, so I still needed some babysitters. Even if you have nothing going on, it's still fine to get someone to watch your son for an hour or two one of those afternoons so you can run out and get some things done or decompress. The point isn't to do every single thing on your own. The point (along with quality time together) is making sure your infant is taken care of without having your wife involved.

Leave on a high note: I took my daughters to MOD pizza, one of those trendy custom-pizza-to-go places, since they love pizza and I could get them food quickly. Plus, it's usually kind of noisy, so if they got fussy no one would notice. They did great, eating more pizza than I did. As soon as I started sensing the tide was turning against me, we left. When you are on your own, it's not a good time time test your kid's limits. Do the activity and leave when they are still smiling.

Maximize the bonding: It's easier to be more mentally checked out when you have two of you to watch your kid. You may find yourself staring at your phone for a bit, or half watching them, half watching the news. When it's just you, why not take advantage of it? Get down on the floor and play with them. Keep the TV off while you're reading a book. Get in the bath and splash around a bit with them. They aren't looking for mommy right now. They are focused on you. How cool is that? That's also the kind of thing that pays off later when they need consoling!

Prepare, prepare, prepare: My wife is excellent at preparing. It's why we make a good team; she knows what to bring, what time we need to be there, and what clothes are where. I'm good at getting all the kids down to bed and coming up with creative solutions to problems. When she's out of town, though, I need to wear both hats. I'll confess — I hadn't thought ahead about how many diapers we had left before I left for work, and we just barely had enough to get through! It was a good reminder, and from that point on, I double-checked the diaper bag and other items so that I had everything I needed.

Get out of the house: It's tempting to stay in when you're alone with your kid, especially a baby. I strongly suggest you fight that urge and get out. Go to a park with a stroller. Go to the grocery store with a baby carrier. It makes the time go by faster and helps limit frustrations that can mount when you're isolated and stuck in one place.

Having one-on-one time with your little kid is really fun ... and intense. But you can do it. Let me know how it goes!

15

Why all of this matters so much right away.

You don't get a "redo" as a parent. Otherwise, I would be hitting that button constantly.

My wife and I play a game on road trips called "Truth or Truth."

The rules are straightforward. There is no "dare" option, so you're gonna get a dose of honesty either way. It helps the time fly by.

Well, that, and the other long road trip aide we added. We entered a parent cheat code installed a fold-down DVD player/screen in our minivan. It's a lifesaver. No worries about kids messing with an iPad or fighting over who is watching what. We pick one movie and we're set. I highly recommend it. And you get to listen to a bunch of old Disney movies and realize how strange the dialogue is!

But "Truth or Truth" is just for us.

Sample questions:

- "What country would you move to if you had to choose right now?"
- "What dead celebrity would you have lunch with if you could?"
- "Who would you sleep with on _____ show?" (Pick a show, any show!)

But sometimes we ask each other about what we'd do differently if we could in different scenarios.

From our childhood: I'd tell myself not to worry about being popular because most of the kids who were popular in middle school didn't end up having great lives after all!

From our 20s: Good Lord, we'd redo so many things.

From the time we became parents: Where do I start? Not enforcing naptime? Not taking advantage of the non-crawling stage?

The thing is, you can think back and do an *It's a Wonderful Life* or *A Christmas Carol* to think about how life would be different if you did this or that, or if you weren't there at all. If you spent too many parties not talking to anyone and regretting how isolated you are, you can make that change at the very next party and force yourself to start a conversation. If you never went for that dream career, you can sign up for classes today to go after that degree, or send a resume to that ideal employer.

When you're thinking of regrets with how you take care of your kid, though?

What you did has already made an impact, and you can't undo things so easily.

For dads who took too long to get involved, they can try to make up ground as your baby gets older, but, to quote that rock doctor guy in *Frozen*, "The heart is not so easily changed."

Your baby starts making a bond on the first day. The first minute, actually! That's why attachment parenting experts promote skin-to-skin contact as soon as possible with both parents. Your baby starts making a connection. They've been listening to your voice from inside the womb, so when they are born, they already recognize you.

Dads who are doing "kangaroo care" (skin-to-skin) get a great shot at forming that bond. Dads who keep putting off any real involvement for whatever reason will likely get frustrated later on when that now-young boy or girl isn't listening to them. Why would they? The dad didn't put in the time.

I want dads to realize how precious that time is in those early stages. It will fly by so fast and if you aren't careful, that baby will turn into a toddler who hasn't really connected with him.

And what would be the end result? More responsibility on your shoulders! Your kid will keep turning to you again and again to be their emotional support and solve their problems because you were the only one who was there in the beginning. And that problem compounds. The more he turns away from dad, the less dad feels like he can make any difference, which means the kid turns to you more, and the cycle continues.

With two parents involved, your baby will feel like she can turn to either of you. When you're at the end of your rope, you need that balance. It's not like your baby will sense that you need a break! That's where having equally invested parents pays off. If instead, your partner spent the first year or two avoiding scenarios where he had to soothe your crying baby or stay up all night to help them sleep, it would stand to reason your kid will have a tough time feeling like your partner can all of a sudden be a soothing presence later on.

There are real consequences to passing off the baby every

time things aren't perfect. There is an impact to spending days on end offering no more than a pat on the head and a series of "uh huhs" to an infant who wants affection and attention, even if your battery is on one bar.

I've seen it first hand.

How I tried (and failed).

I tried to be an involved dad in those early years with my kids, and I'd be the first to say at times, I sucked more times than I'd like to admit.

I would get drained from work or my commute, so instead of reading an extra book or doing some tummy time with my son, I'd just go through the motions and get him to bed. I'd get frustrated if he didn't want to fall asleep quickly because I was exhausted, rather than appreciate that his schedule doesn't always coincide with what works best for me.

Other days, yes, I'd babywear the hell out of him and it was great. My wife would come home to me steam cleaning all the carpets with my son strapped to my chest (efficiency!), and I'd feel like I'd be having an A+ dad day.

Or, later on, I'd take all of our kids for an extended walk with the stroller and answer all their questions and sing funny songs with them. Good days. Felt nice!

I can't redo those hours I spent staring at my phone. The days I went through the motions. The months that flew by without me appreciating the "lasts." As they say, you don't know when the last time your baby will do something until it's already happened.

I didn't know at the time it would be the last time my son needed me to rock him to sleep. If I did, I would have hit the "redo" button on the nights of rocking where I was more focused on getting him to fall asleep fast than feeling those tiny fingers curl around me and his slow breathing on my chest.

I can promise you that your partner is not thinking of this stuff often.

We are task-focused. It's what project can we complete, like building the crib or putting up baby gates.

The what, not the how.

Make it a point to take a breath together and think of what your baby or infant is doing. Not how it impacts what you need to do next, but how you want to *react* to it. If they start crawling, appreciate it for what it is. Right now, make it clear it's OK if your partner doesn't jump right into baby-proofing the house. He can take the time to get on his belly and soak it in.

Because if he's not careful, he'll spend that stage easily getting frustrated by a baby gate not installing correctly or what to do with that glass coffee table that's now a danger, and not on what your baby needs in that moment. They need a dad who is helping them explore in a safe way!

Dads are amazing at looking out for their babies. But they don't get a redo on the emotional stuff. Focusing on the right thing at the right moment makes a huge difference.

I know I'm guilty of focusing on the wrong things with the best intentions. And because it looks to the outside world like I was doing "dad stuff," nobody bats an eye. I was helping! But what that doesn't show is whether I was making a difference with my kid. I got frustrated with things that weren't worth it in the name of solving a problem. I was being a problem solver when my son or daughters needed a dad.

I can get a do-over on my approach to middle school. These days, I haven't given nearly as much thought on what people think of me ... that's freeing!

But parenting? All I can do is be the best dad I can be today. And tomorrow. And every day after that. All your partner can do is make the effort the next time to take that breath and appreciate your baby's stage and development without immediately trying to "fix it."

You can do amazing work together as parents. Don't over-think it. Your kid is incredibly lucky to have you. I can't wait to hear how it goes.

Acknowledgements

I'd like to sincerely thank my wife, first and foremost. I would not have been able to write this book without her, not to mention be a father in the first place. Her incredible patience, kindness, and dedication makes every day as a dad that much easier.

Thank you to the many people who read a chapter or three of this book in its earlier versions so I could gather feedback, as well as all the fathers who offered stories and insights that helped me get a better understanding of how my experience connected with their own.

Thank you to Fe Amarante for not only the beautiful cover art, but for pushing me to keep working on this book.

Thank you to all those who listened to me talk endlessly about this project, from writing to marketing, for many months longer than any of us expected. I have such a supportive community that wanted me to help make this a reality.

Additional Resources

I've found these resources are fantastic for helping new dads! In addition to http://instafather.com, please have your partner check out:

- Dad 2.0: This annual summit for dad blogger and fathers in general also has a wonderful and supportive online community.
- Fatherly: One of the best blogs out there for dad-related issues.
- Scary Mommy: They have a wealth of funny stories (I even wrote about getting a vasectomy!), as well as stories that will help your partner get a better idea what kind of things you stress about.

Enjoy *The New Mom's Guide to New Dads*? Use #newmoms-guidetonewdads on social media and tag @instafatherandy! I'd love to see your feedback or a photo of you with the book and your baby!

About the book

"What in the hell is that man that got me pregnant thinking?"
— Paraphrased quote from many a bewildered new mom.

You've been reading everything in sight about what to expect as a new mom — "Should I breastfeed or use formula?"; "Do we vaccinate right away?"; "Oh God, is eating the placenta a thing now?"

But what you've been desperately looking for is a guide that tells you what to do to help your partner figure out fatherhood because he's kinda driving you crazy and you need more help. Sure, there are a few books out there by dads, to dads. But you and I both know that dude you had a baby with is not the best at sharing his feelings and seeking help, let alone telling you he's freaked out about fatherhood.

Enter *The New Mom's Guide to New Dads*. Get enlightening, humorous-yet-useful insight into what guys are anxious about and what moms can do to maximize their partner's fatherhood potential. Flat out, more dads need to step up (and when they do, they'll realize how amazing it is to be an involved parent). Andrew Shaw, a father of three young children and an award-winning parenting columnist, is shining a light on what is often holding guys back from being the kind of dad you can shamelessly brag about to friends, as well as help you feel less stress.

About the Author

Andrew Shaw is an award-winning parenting columnist and journalist and creator of Instafather, a blog dedicated to helping new parents, especially dads. He lives in Pennsylvania with his wife, son and twin daughters. In between constantly getting these kids snacks, he's a marketing strategist and a professional improv comedian who has toured across the mid-Atlantic. Andrew's work has been featured on SCARY MOMMY, THE GOOD MEN PROJECT, FATHERLY and CENTRAL PENN PARENT.

You can connect with me on:
- http://instafather.com
- http://twitter.com/instafatherandy
- http://facebook.com/instafatherandy